Real Life Financial Planning

An Easy-to-Understand System to Organize Your Financial Plan and Prioritize Financial Decisions

3rd EDITION

Todd D. Bramson, CFP®, ChFC, CLU

ASPATORE

Mat #40917851

ISBN 978-0-314-23290-8

For corrections, updates, comments, or any other inquiries please e-mail
TLR.AspatoreEditorial@thomson.com.

First Printing, 2004
10 9 8 7 6 5 4 3 2 1

ASPATORE

Aspatore Books, a Thomson Reuters business, exclusively publishes C-Level executives (CEO, CFO, CTO, CMO, Partner) from the world's most respected companies and law firms. C-Level Business Intelligence™, as conceptualized and developed by Aspatore Books, provides professionals of all levels with proven business intelligence from industry insiders—direct and unfiltered insight from those who know it best—as opposed to third-party accounts offered by unknown authors and analysts. Aspatore Books is committed to publishing an innovative line of business and legal books, those which lay forth principles and offer insights that, when employed, can have a direct financial impact on the reader's business objectives, whatever they may be. In essence, Aspatore publishes critical tools for all business professionals.

Additional books in the *Real Life* book series

Real Life Financial Planning
(second printing)

Real Life Financial Planning for Young Dentists
(second printing)

Real Life Financial Planning for the High Income Specialist

Real Life Financial Planning for Young Lawyers

Real Life Financial Planning with Case Studies
(second printing)

Real Life Financial Planning with Case Studies
(featuring Langdon Ford Financial)

Real Life Money Management for Pharmacists

Real Life Financial Planning for the New Physician
(third printing)

Real Life Financial Planning for the Medical Professional

Real Life Financial Planning with Case Studies for Women

Real Life Financial Planning for the Student-Athlete

Dedications

This book is dedicated to my immediate family: my parents David and Fran, my wife and best friend Jerilyn, my children Ali and David, and my sister Julie. Also, to all relatives, in-laws, and extended family who enrich our personal life. Without the love, support, and guidance of all of these people, I wouldn't have learned the most important lesson of life: "When all is said and done, it is the quality and depth of relationships and experiences that are the essence of life...not the accumulation of material possessions."

Thank You

I extend a special thank-you to...

...my clients who have trusted me with their financial decisions.

...my staff, partners, and business associates who make work a pleasure.

...Greg Halat and Somer Mansur for helping me and my clients.

...all of those special people who I have learned from, especially Dick and Kathy Anderson, Ed Deutschlander, John Gadow, Kevin Hogan, Joel Huth, Dick Koob, Bob Logas, Phil Richards, Scott Richards, Mark Schweiger, Dave Smrecek, Nick Stevens, Dave Vasos, Diane Yohn, Pete and Jody Witte, and lifelong friends Andy, Brad, Dan, Jeff, Pete, and Scott.

Lastly, a special thank-you to Mishelle Shepard, who kept encouraging and helping me throughout the process of writing the first edition of this book. This would still be handwritten ideas on a yellow scratch pad if it weren't for you. "Who would have known back then that *Real Life Financial Planning* would grow into a successful book series?"

Real Life Financial Planning

CONTENTS

	PREFACE	9
1	THE BASIC QUESTIONS	11
2	WHERE DO I START?	17
3	THE PYRAMID	25
4	THE SECURITY AND CONFIDENCE STAGE	31
5	THE CAPITAL ACCUMULATION STAGE	39
6	THE TAX-ADVANTAGED STAGE	45
7	529 COLLEGE SAVINGS PLANS	61
8	THE SPECULATION STAGE	67
9	FREQUENTLY ASKED QUESTIONS	69
10	CASE STUDIES	75
11	ADDITIONAL RESOURCES	97
	ABOUT THE AUTHOR	103

Tax Disclosure

This information is a general discussion of the relevant federal tax laws. It is not intended for, nor can it be used by any taxpayer for, the purpose of avoiding federal tax penalties. This information is provided to support the promotion or marketing of ideas that may benefit a taxpayer. Taxpayers should seek the advice of their own tax and legal advisors regarding any tax and legal issues applicable to their specific circumstances.

Preface

I have gained wisdom, strength of character, integrity, empathy, and the value of giving by my parents' example. Unfortunately, my father passed away very suddenly at the age of forty-five, when I was just sixteen. It was three weeks from the day he discovered a few black and blue marks on his arms to the day he died of acute leukemia. In this short time, we never had a chance to talk about the future, although I feel his guidance through my conscience and in the wisdom of others, including my mother.

It is interesting how the experiences of childhood, both good and bad, mold the path we follow as adults. My dad did not have much life insurance, or any established relationships with trusted advisors. When he died, my mother was lost financially. She was given very poor financial advice, and the small amount of life insurance she had was lost in an unsuitable and inappropriate investment. My family's misfortune defined my passion. It was through this unfortunate situation that I became empowered. My mission has remained intact for over thirty years, as I decided this would never happen to my family or anyone who entrusted me with their important financial decisions.

Due to our significant financial crisis, I became eligible for an Evans Scholarship. In the early 1930s, Chick Evans became a nationally ranked golfer and started a college scholarship program with his earnings instead of turning pro. This scholarship has now grown to the largest privately funded scholarship in the country. There are over 800 students currently benefiting from it, as well as over 8,500 alumni. His vision and generosity have been an inspiration to me.

With that in mind, this book is my benevolence. I am now in the fortunate position of being able to give back. Some of the proceeds from this book will be given to charity, including the Evans Scholars Foundation, the Breakfast Optimist Foundation, the MDRT Foundation, the Madison Community Foundation, the Leukemia Society, and many others. I am interested in "partnering" with other charities to help in their fundraising efforts, and I encourage you to contact me to discuss those possibilities.

I'd like to share a proverb containing some valuable wisdom and insight:

He (or She!) who knows, and knows he knows, is wise;
Follow him.
He who knows, but knows not that he knows, is asleep;
Awaken him.
He who knows not, and knows he does not know, is simple;
Teach him.
He who knows not, but does not know that he knows not, is dangerous;
Avoid him.

I believe it is our mission in life to listen to and learn from, or **follow**, those who fall into the first category. But it is also our mission to take our unique gifts and make them available to those who are asleep or simple by **awakening** and **teaching** them. Also, time is too precious to spend with those who are dangerous. **Avoid** and minimize the amount of time you spend with people who fall into this category, and your enjoyment of life will multiply. We all have unique gifts and abilities, and to the extent that our lives overlap and intertwine, we can all grow together carrying out our unique visions.

It is my hope that this book will educate and help you to achieve all of your personal and financial goals.

Todd D. Bramson
October 2009
Madison, WI

1

The Basic Questions

Why the Title "Real Life Financial Planning"?

I have spent almost twenty-eight years working directly with individuals on their financial plans and financial planning questions. There is so much information to be found…but sometimes not much wisdom. Hopefully this book summarizes the wisdom I have learned and shared with my clients in individual meetings throughout the years. *Real Life Financial Planning* is simply a practical method of understanding, organizing, and prioritizing financial decisions.

Most financial planning publications and financial plans themselves assume everyone lives a long, healthy life and saves a good portion of their income in quality investments that always do well. This book addresses all of the issues that happen in real life, and I hope you take the time to read this and work with a trained professional to develop a financial plan that meets *your* goals and objectives.

Why Is There an Ever-Increasing Number of Financial Planning Books on the Market Today?

Because there is an ever-increasing need to get educated.

- Few parents openly discuss financial matters with their children while they're growing up.
- Personal financial planning is rarely a subject taught in school.

- Many young people today begin their professional life already in the red when you consider that the average student who takes out a college student loan graduates with over $20,000 in debt.
- We live high-pressure, busy lifestyles that don't allow much free time to try to learn about all of the options we have.

These unfortunate facts mean there are far too many people today who are ill equipped to deal with the practical and fundamental necessities of planning for a secure and independent financial life.

Times have changed. Today, more than ever, your financial future needs you. Long gone are the days when you could rely on your company to pay back decades of loyal service with a comfortable pension plan. This is even more evident as we learn that some of America's largest companies report that their pension plans are underfunded. Many loyal lifelong employees are going to be surprised, and even shocked, when their financial security is in jeopardy.

Even the government can't assure you of a reasonable retirement after a lifetime of Social Security contributions. Of course, Social Security was never designed to be the primary income for retirees. In addition, financial products have become increasingly complex, and we are continually inundated with confusing financial information.

These facts aren't meant to stress you out, but to wake you up to the financial reality of America today. It's not simply a matter of whether you will be able to retire rich, but whether you will simply be able to sustain your current lifestyle for the rest of your life.

Don't wait another day. This book is meant to give you an introduction into the often-intimidating world of financial planning. You will learn of the varieties of investments and insurance options. You will begin to understand some terminology, and get advice on where to go next, whether you intend to go the road alone or get some help along the way. Best of all, you will climb the pyramid of financial success.

Financial success isn't, as most people might suspect, the ability to make one or two decisions that turn a buck into a million. Rather, financial success is the result of many small but sound decisions that, when compounded, add up to substantial financial security.

You are in complete control. Or at least you should be. When it comes to spending and saving, investing and paying taxes, many may offer good advice, but you're the only one who can do anything about it. Maybe you're a chronic shopper. Maybe you're unsure of your investment options and how to prioritize them. Maybe you don't have a clue where your paycheck goes each month. In any case, if you're reading this book, you already understand the importance of getting your future under control, and that's the crucial first step to financial freedom.

Who Needs a Financial Planner?

Financial independence and the accumulation of wealth are no accident. Granted, it's not possible to plan for every single event in life, but even tragedy can feel more manageable when you are financially prepared for it. *If you're like many people, you probably spend more time planning for a vacation than for your entire financial future!* Whether it's preparing for the future, securing yourself and your family against tragedy, or planning for the good times, your money deserves your undivided attention.

Car accidents, marriage, divorce, kids, corporate downsizing, death, and retirement, for better or worse, are the realities of life. Planning for any circumstance, both happy and sad, may seem like a burden right now, but the right planning will rescue you when (not if) unforeseen circumstances arise. Sometimes, solid planning can even turn otherwise bad fortune into good—maybe that downsizing could lead to a better job, or the divorce to a healthier situation, or the large credit card bill finally gives you the motivation to curb your spending and live on a budget.

The truth is, we all need to plan for our financial futures. So the question is not whether to plan, but how to go about making a plan, and whether we need a professional to help. The information age has complicated the field of financial planning. It is interesting to consider that twenty years ago financial news may have made top headlines two or three times throughout the year when the stock market would do particularly poorly or well, or if there was some other major economic news. Today, however, we have news programs dedicated to nothing else 24-7, and the number of financial headlines in the daily papers can be overwhelming. Still, there is a big difference between information and wisdom, and that's where the insight of a trusted professional can help.

Several situations that may call for a financial planner's expertise are:

- *You are a professional without much spare time.* If you're working for a large company, they may provide the groundwork for investing wisely for the long term, but even the best can't take into consideration the special circumstances of each individual or family. In this case, a financial planner can save you a bit of your most precious commodity—time.

- *You are easily bored or overwhelmed by financial questions.* If, for example, preparing a budget is such a nuisance that you can't even imagine having to sort through anything more complex, like insurance options, trends in mutual funds, or the stock market, then hiring a financial planner may be money well spent for greater peace of mind.

- *You are considering a complicated set of employee benefits in combination with personally owned insurance and investments.* You certainly don't want a new employer (or an existing employer who has changed their benefit structure) to conflict or overlap with your current investments. Such gaps or possible duplications should be examined thoroughly.

- *You are recently divorced or have lost a spouse who had previously been the one handling financial affairs for the household.* As if dealing with the trauma of divorce or death is not enough, being thrust into unknown financial waters without a trusted advisor can make you feel like you're trying to stay afloat with bricks chained to your ankles.

- *You have recently graduated from high school, college, or graduate school and are suddenly expected to become financially independent.* The saying "An ounce of prevention beats a pound of cure" is an important one in the world of financial planning. Seemingly insurmountable debt plagues the future of many young people. Learning to budget properly, to choose from insurance options, and to make wise investments are necessary life skills. Getting professional advice now beats paying for costly mistakes later.

- *You are self-employed.* In this case, you most likely have to "wear many hats" as an entrepreneur. You are in manufacturing, sales, marketing, accounting, and customer servicing, and probably don't have time to investigate or be aware of the many planning options available to you for you and your employees. A financial planner can help you sort through the many issues facing you.

As much as some of us would like to leave it all up to a professional, it's crucial that you understand the basics. A financial advisor is someone there to educate and advise you and assist you in taking action to develop a plan, but ultimately the final decisions are yours. A good financial planner will educate you as to the options you face, acting as a teacher, so that you understand all of the relevant issues. Then you can work together to create a plan, and monitor it over the years. A successful financial plan is an ongoing process that stays up to date with your situation.

There are many sides to most issues. The topic doesn't matter, whether it's religion, politics, stocks, insurance, sales loads, or how to finance your house...just to name a few. There are always many individual considerations, and the correct solution depends on a variety of factors. I get leery of advice that suggests you should "always" do this or "never" do that. I believe life is far more gray than it is black and white.

I am not the first to say this, and I certainly won't be the last: "It is crucial to trust your own judgment and instincts before taking action, no matter how good someone makes their argument." The best way to gain confidence in your own better judgment is to educate yourself on the topic at hand.

With that in mind, in this book, you'll find general guidance to the most important financial questions facing everyone:

- How much money should I have in emergency reserves?
- In which order should I go about paying off my debts?
- Which is the right kind of insurance for me, and how much do I need?

- What are the most common financial mistakes people make?
- When should I maximize contributions to retirement plans?
- What is the best mortgage to take out?

...and many more!

If you don't know the answers yet, don't worry. Just keep reading, because you're about to find out.

2

Where Do I Start?

Your Net Worth Statement

The starting point of any financial plan is to figure out your current net worth. This is a snapshot of what you are worth at an exact point in time. To determine your net worth, you simply add up all of your assets and subtract all of your liabilities (debts). Sometimes, when you are just starting out, the net worth is actually a negative number because the liabilities exceed the assets.

To measure your financial progress, it is important to know your net worth. Many people measure their financial progress by how much money they have in the bank. In reality, as the value of your assets go up, such as a house, business, or investments, and as you pay debts down, your net worth may be increasing more dramatically than you think. The most important way to measure financial progress is to calculate your net worth regularly.

Don't panic! Here's where we have to get just a bit technical. Before you shake your head and think, "Whoa, this looks way too involved for me," just try taking it one step at a time, following the chart and example on page 19. After you learn how to do it once, it'll be just like riding a bike.

In simple terms, what would you be worth if you sold everything you owned and turned it into cash, then paid off all your debts? If this is the first time you're preparing a net worth statement, it's also a good idea to try to estimate what you think your net worth has been over the last few years. Hopefully you will be pleasantly surprised at the progress you've made.

There are several categories within the net worth statement.

Fixed assets is the first category. Fixed assets are those assets that do not have a risk of a loss of principal. These would include the most conservative accounts you can invest in. A few examples would be checking and savings accounts, money market accounts, certificates of deposit, T-bills, EE savings bonds, and whole life (non-variable) insurance cash values. These would be assets you have access to in an emergency. They are available now, and therefore are considered liquid.

Variable assets include most other financial assets. Examples include stocks, bonds, mutual funds, retirement plans, or any investment where the principal can fluctuate. Besides that, there is a potential for a higher overall rate of return on these assets (with greater return potential), and they are useful for the income and growth components of your longer-term financial planning. Please know that investments will fluctuate and, when redeemed, may be worth more or less than when originally invested.

Your *personal and other assets* would include tangible assets such as your house, personal or business property, and vehicles. Other tangible assets, such as a stereo, computer, or camera, would also be included here.

Don't get too bogged down trying to establish a value for every piece of personal property. You may already have that information available from your homeowner's or renter's insurance policies, but if not, a rough estimate will work just fine. The main reason for gathering this information is to have an estimate so you can monitor trends. This way, when you are reviewing your net worth after some time, you will be able to track how this category has changed or account for some of the money you spent.

Sample Net Worth Statement

Fixed Assets:

Savings Account:	$5,000
Checking Account:	$3,000
Certificate of Deposit:	$2,000
Total Fixed Assets:	**$10,000**

Variable Assets:

IRA:	$3,000
Mutual Funds:	$5,000
Individual Stocks:	$2,000
Variable Life Cash Value:	$4,000
401k Balance:	$20,000
Total Variable Assets:	**$34,000**

Personal and Other Assets:

Home:	$200,000
Vehicle:	$20,000
Personal Property	$20,000
Total Personal and Other:	**$240,000**

Total Assets:	**$284,000**

Liabilities:

Mortgage:	$160,000
Home Equity Line of Credit:	$5,000
Vehicle Loan:	$10,000
Credit Cards:	$2,000

Total Liabilities:	**$177,000**

Net Worth (Assets minus Liabilities):	**$107,000**

Tip: Use a camera or, better yet, a video camera to tape each room in your house, including closets and the garage. In the event of a loss, it will be much easier to remember for insurance companies' reporting purposes.

For your liabilities, list the amount you owe if you could pay off the amount today, not the total of the payments over time, which would include interest. Subtract your total liabilities from your assets to arrive at your net worth. If you're like many people, this can be a sobering experience. Don't forget to include all loans, like mortgages, auto loans, credit cards, student loans, personal debts, and consumer debt.

If you are young and/or just starting out in the work world, don't feel too upset if you learn your net worth is negative. For many people in the first stages of financial planning, it is the seemingly unmanageable debt that whips their spending habits into shape and pushes them to start planning for the future. It is also not unusual for recent graduates or those who have just finished some form of job training or other education to have a negative net worth because of high student loan debt. However, remember that education is not a needless expense, and it should be considered an investment in your financial future. In fact, taking on debt to finance an education, a real estate purchase, or a business is an investment in your future, which should help you increase your net worth in the future. Consumer debt, when out of control, is what needs to be monitored and paid off immediately.

If you fit into the negative net worth category, your first financial goal is to get your new worth back to zero. For you, it is especially important to establish a financial plan and get control of your financial life as soon as possible. But instead of dreading the process, have some fun with it. I suggest that clients throw themselves an "I'm Worthless Party" after they've worked hard to achieve their "$0" net worth. (Just don't put the party on a credit card you can't pay off next month!)

Ignore the urge to put your head in the sand, thinking you have no power over the situation. *You are not alone, and there's no reason to be embarrassed.* To prove it, you can take a look at our government. Their high federal deficit sets a dangerous precedent not only for our culture, but also the world's economy. No matter how big your debt problem, it looks relatively small in this light!

Simply make up your mind now to reverse the situation, and be proud that you're taking the right steps. The obvious way to improve your net worth is to decrease your spending and/or increase your income and savings. Begin by taking a serious look at your spending habits, and make sure you are doing everything you can to achieve, first a zero, and eventually a positive net worth. Getting yourself back to financial stability may feel like a long and lonely road, but with the help of a financial planner, you at least don't have to feel like you're going at it alone. Or why not "buddy up" like people do when they work out. Find a friend who is also motivated to get their financial act in order, and educate yourselves and build your net worth together. After a while, being frugal, saving and investing, and getting on top of your finances becomes addicting.

The Millionaire Next Door by Thomas Stanley outlines some benchmark figures for what your net worth should be at any given time, age, or stage in life. I'd encourage you to read that book for an in-depth study of very successful people. Your net worth represents your financial security and, ultimately, financial independence. So of course, the closer you are to retirement, the higher your net worth should be. A successful financial plan achieves one's maximum net worth, works under the most difficult circumstances, and maximizes the enjoyment of your wealth. It will also be important to insure yourself against unforeseen tragedies and to consider whether you want to leave an inheritance to your family or your favorite charity, creating a legacy that lives on forever.

In summary, the most critical starting point to a financial plan is evaluating your net worth. Then, on a periodic basis, you can compare the results in order to establish trends and measure improvement. A convenient time to do this is once a year when you're doing your taxes. This way, all the paperwork is readily available and you're focused on your annual earnings and expenditures anyway. Keep all the financial records together from each year's tax forms and net worth calculations for easy reference.

Your Budget

After calculating your net worth, you'll want to look at your monthly budget and define exactly where your money is being spent. The categories of the monthly budget should also include any deductions from your paycheck, like state and federal income taxes, Social Security, and employee benefits. Once you have your take-home pay, you should deduct all of the fixed expenses and the estimated variable expenses.

Are you unable to account for where a large portion of your money goes? This is the case for many people. To overcome it, try a few or all of the following tips:

- Carry a pocket calendar with you for three months, and record every cent you spend, no matter if it's for a candy bar or a cup of coffee, or the mortgage and car payment. Then tally it up and categorize it at the end of each month. (Some software programs, like *Quicken*, make this very easy. Well…maybe not easy, but at least helpful. This process takes some time, but is well worth it if you are a spender.)

- Vow to go back to the days of cash-only transactions. For everything other than your large monthly payments (and even those, if you want to get really serious), stop using your debit and credit cards or writing checks for day-to-day expenditures like groceries, drugstore items, clothing, and so on. It feels much different when you have to shell out $50 cash for a purchase rather than handing over a piece of plastic.

- Treat your savings account or investment amount as a bill you pay out every month like any other. Experience has shown that if you don't get in the habit of saving money on a regular basis, either through a payroll deduction or an automatic withdrawal from your checking account, the money you intended to go toward savings or investments is mysteriously spent elsewhere.

How quickly you can move toward financial security depends on how motivated you are to save money. It's not easy for Americans to live on less than their income, considering our shopping and credit-loving culture. However, if you start early enough, saving 15 percent of your gross income will typically be enough to keep you safe from financial worries later on. If you are getting a later start, you may need to be living on 75 to 80 percent of your income and saving 20 to 25 percent!

Keep in mind that saving or investing 15 percent means you are able to live on 85 percent of your income. As elementary as this may sound, the significance is critical. In later years, this savings could accumulate to a substantial sum if invested properly. Also, it will teach you how to live below your means—a financial goal that seemingly every expert agrees upon, but few Americans live by.

3

The Pyramid

If you took a one thousand-piece puzzle and dumped all the pieces on the table, it is initially a daunting task to begin to put the puzzle together. Take a puzzle piece out of the pile at random, and it's hard to know where that piece fits into the big picture. It is much easier to put the puzzle together if you have a picture of what the scene will look like once completed. So you look at the picture on the box to give you a guide to what the puzzle looks like when completed. I designed the pyramid as a method of seeing how a properly designed financial plan looks when it is put together correctly. Once you understand that, specific decisions are easier because everything is in perspective.

The pyramid is a method of explaining the financial planning concept by categorizing your financial plan into stages. Of course, individual goals, habits, accomplishments, and so on are all unique, but most people share the same fundamental life stages. As a simple method of efficiently organizing your financial life, the pyramid represents the key to financial independence, and demonstrates the basic goal of increasing your assets and reducing your debt in order to have enough money invested to retire comfortably. Individuals may place more or less importance on one section of the pyramid than another, which is perfectly acceptable.

Without a doubt, organizing your finances in order to build a solid base is the first step. If you do this, you may be subjecting your financial situation to undue risk, which will cause problems later on. On the other hand, it's also important not to place too much emphasis on only one stage, neglecting the overall balance. This could be a sign of being overly conservative. As an example, not taking advantage of higher potential returns in equity (stock) investments may mean losing your purchasing power in the long run, because the dollars may be worth less due to the effects of taxes and inflation.

It is very important to try to accomplish a lifelong financial balance. You certainly don't want to get to the age of sixty-five with a huge amount of money saved up, only to be in poor health and not be able to enjoy it, especially if that means you scrimped and saved your whole life and worked so hard that you didn't enjoy yourself along the way. By the same token, you don't want to be nearing retirement and realize you haven't saved enough and now must take a substantial drop in your standard of living or go back to work to simply survive. The ideal situation would be to retire at the same or a greater standard of living than you were accustomed to in your working years, but not feel at any time that you have greatly sacrificed.

As mentioned in Chapter 2, a fundamental of short- and long-term financial success is living on less than your income. If you can get used to living on 80 to 90 percent of your income, this allows you to commit 10 to 20 percent of your income to your net worth. Initially, this may mean aggressively paying of loans, but over time, the majority of this extra income should be saved. If you are living paycheck to paycheck, is there a way you can decrease your expenses and/or increase your income so you can start building some surplus funds into your monthly budget?

As you can see by the diagram below, there are four main stages to the financial planning pyramid: the *Security and Confidence Stage*, the *Capital Accumulation Stage*, the *Tax-Advantaged Stage*, and the *Speculation Stage*.

PYRAMID OF FINANCIAL NEEDS

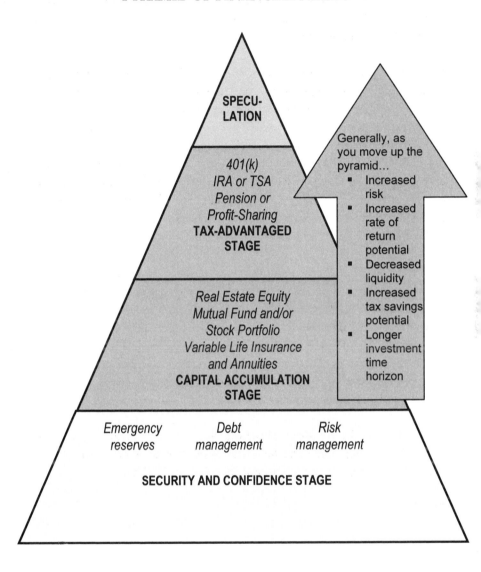

The ideal investment is completely liquid and has lots of tax advantages, a great rate of return, and low risk. If you find an advisor or salesperson claiming to have such an investment, you would be wise to walk, no, run away. This ideal investment does not exist.

Let's use an analogy of spinning plates. If you have ever been to a circus or seen a juggler (the Peking acrobats), you may have seen a performer attempt to spin many plates on top of long sticks…all at the same time. The objective is to take limited energy, and allocate it in such a manner as to keep all the plates spinning. It doesn't do any good to devote a lot of time to one spinning plate while the others are slowing down, wobbling, and falling down. The goal is to keep all the plates spinning!

Your financial plan is on somewhat the same level, with each financial decision representing a different plate. First, you need to find out which plates you want to start spinning, and then direct your dollars to keep them going. You could have several debt reduction plates, some risk management (insurance) plates, retirement and/or college education plates, and so on. Each individual situation is going to be different. Again, there are limited resources that need to be allocated in such a way as to accomplish all of your goals. This is where the advice of a professional and experienced financial advisor can be very valuable. You can call me a financial juggler.

The key financial variables in the pyramid are risk, liquidity, rate of return, and tax advantages. The money in your emergency reserves and at the *Security and Confidence Stage* should be very liquid or accessible. Generally, as you move to higher stages in the pyramid, the less liquid your funds become.

Risk and rate of return tend to go hand in hand. The higher the amount of risk you take, the higher the rate of return should be…given time. In the pyramid, typically lower risk and lower rates of return should be at the base of your planning, with risk and rate of return increasing as you move up the pyramid. Historically, stock market and investing returns become more predictable the longer the timeframe that is considered. Keep in mind, however, that past performance is not indicative of future results. Investments will fluctuate and, when redeemed, could be worth more or less than when originally invested.

From a tax standpoint, there are typically not too many tax advantages at the lower level. If you have money in a savings account, that money is generating ordinary income on which you are paying tax, so there are no tax advantages there. On the other hand, when you put money into a qualified retirement plan, the contribution is on a before-tax basis, delaying and deferring the tax to a later date. Under most circumstances, however, you cannot touch the money in your qualified plan until age fifty-nine and a half without paying a 10 percent early withdrawal penalty, plus the income taxes due on that amount. The rule of thumb on tax savings is similar to risk and rate of return. As you move up the pyramid, you'll have greater tax advantages on your investments.

A Discussion of Risk

There is no such thing as a risk-free investment. Even a savings account is not risk-free. Let me explain. Risk is commonly discussed in terms of loss of principal. This is market risk. Most recently, during the recent bear markets of 2000–2001 and 2007–2009 (a period of downturn in the stock market), many investors lost some of the value of their investment if they owned stocks and/or stock mutual funds. There are other forms of risk besides market risk.

Purchasing Power Risk: Another term for this is inflation. If the cost for products and services rises faster than the interest rate being credited on your savings and checking accounts, you are exposed to purchasing power risk. While you don't lose any principal, you are still losing ground relative to inflation. This is a particular problem currently for retirees who have traditionally held CDs (bank certificates of deposit) and lived off the interest each year.

Interest Rate Risk: Bonds and fixed income securities are subject to this risk. Your principal value can decline if interest rates climb quickly. The severity of the loss is often magnified by the duration and/or maturity of the bonds and the credit quality, as well as how quickly interest rates rise. At this time, when interest rates are near forty-year lows, many people who own fixed income securities are unknowingly subjecting their investments to interest rate risk.

Business Risk: This is the risk of losing money due to circumstances out of your control. A business could go bankrupt, and your investment becomes worthless.

Liquidity Risk: This is the risk associated with being invested in real estate, limited partnerships, businesses, and other investments where there is sometimes no immediate market for your value. This is problematic if you have a need for cash and you cannot sell or liquidate your shares. You would invest in something like this only if you had sufficient assets available besides this investment.

Regulatory Risk: Investors run the risk that government policy decisions or influences of society as a whole could endanger an investment's value. Environmental and tax legislation can have a dramatic impact on certain investment values, up or down. It is important to note this risk when investing.

Currency Risk: An investment in international securities can be affected by foreign exchange rate changes, political and economic instability, as well as differences in accounting standards.

Diversity Risk: This will be discussed at length later in the book, but allow me to overstate the obvious...DIVERSIFY!

In summary, a properly structured financial plan will balance all of these variables so that you are diversified by asset class, risk levels, tax treatment, and time horizon.

4

The Security and Confidence Stage

This stage is divided into three main sections, with an emphasis on building up emergency reserves, making sure debt is under control, and taking care of risk management (insurance) needs. Each of these factors is equally important. Most people agree on the need to have money accessible for emergencies, to pay their debts, especially on high-interest credit cards, and to be adequately insured. The trick to the individual financial plan is to figure out the appropriate level for each of these.

1. Emergency Reserves

The one constant in life is that there will always be surprises. The purpose of an emergency reserve fund is just what it sounds like—money that is very accessible when you really need it. In fact, Will Rogers once said, "I'm not so much concerned about the rate of return on my money, just the return of it!" The main characteristic of an investment in this category would be money that is liquid, yet safely invested so the principal remains intact. The most common mistake people make here is not having adequate reserves or taking undue risk with these funds. This money needs to remain liquid in case of unexpected expenses, like car expenses, home repairs, job loss, or medical emergencies. For most people, the main benefit of having an adequate emergency reserve fund is access to funds when needed. When you are financially prepared for these surprises, they become less stressful and are therefore easier to deal with emotionally. Furthermore, when there is a source of funds for these types of emergencies, you do not have to rely on credit cards or personal unsecured high-interest loans.

As a general rule of thumb, your emergency reserve account would be able to cover at least three months of bills. So, if your monthly expenses are averaging $3,000, your emergency reserve fund should be $9,000. Of course, this is a rough guide, and you may want to consider having a higher emergency reserve if you anticipate a big purchase, such as a car or home. Ideally, you do not want to deplete your emergency reserve completely in order to purchase such items.

It may also be important to consider an *emotional rule of thumb*—at what point would a drop in your emergency reserves make you feel nervous? Or, said another way, what is the minimum level of cash you need to have? This amount differs for everyone, and it should take into consideration the stability of your job, your equity in a home, how large and/or liquid your other investments are, and any large bills or purchases you may be planning. If a large purchase or unexpected expenses do drain your reserves, the emphasis of your financial plan should be to replenish those funds at a higher priority than your other investments.

The typical investments that can be used to hold your emergency reserves would include bank investments, money market funds, and/or insurance cash values. The common theme among these investments is their liquidity and the safety of the principal. If you use a bank for your emergency reserves, typically these funds are in savings accounts and interest-bearing checking accounts, as well as money market funds.

For safety of principal and liquidity, savings accounts are the most common option, but not necessarily the best. Such accounts are insured, so there is no market risk, but lots of purchasing poser risk. But this also means there is typically a lower yield than other investments.

Another option is a CD (certificate of deposit), with a relatively short maturity. The disadvantage to a CD is that the money is tied up for the length of the guarantee period, and removing the funds sooner will result in a penalty. To avoid this problem, it can make sense to stagger your CD maturities so that you always have some that come due every six months or so. Therefore, you can access it if you need to or reinvest if you don't.

A money market mutual fund is often the best choice as an emergency reserve possibility. Many people incorrectly associate the term mutual fund with high risk. However, a mutual fund only has as much risk as the underlying investments it owns. A money market mutual fund pools investors' dollars in the typical mutual fund style, and purchases jumbo CDs through banks, Treasury securities (T-bills), as well as commercial paper. Most money market funds have a check writing privilege, which allows you to write checks against your account, subject to minimums of usually $250 or $500. The rate of return earned on these funds will fluctuate based on the short-term money market, but it is typically competitive with the interest rate at the time.

Investments in a money market fund are neither insured nor guaranteed by the FDIC, or any government agency. Although the fund seeks to preserve the value of your investment at $1.00 per share, it is possible to lose money by investing in the fund. In the fall of 2008, the Reserve Primary Fund did fall to $.97 per share, losing 3 percent of the principal.

Life insurance cash values on permanent policies (i.e., whole life, adjustable life, universal life) can also be important sources of emergency reserve funds. These funds are typically earning a competitive fixed rate of return, and they are accessible. It is usually possible to take out a loan or borrow against your cash value, using it as collateral. Or sometimes you can take an outright withdrawal of this money. Remember, though, that any loans or withdrawals taken will reduce both your policy cash value and death benefit.

A home equity line of credit is another option. If you have equity in your house, and if interest rates are low and these loans are tax-deductible, this option should not be discounted. In fact, in periods of time when interest rates are low, maintaining an open line of credit against your house can be a source of money in an emergency. It could also be used to pay down a high-interest credit card or for a major purchase, like a car. The drawback is that it needs to be paid off when you sell your house, which of course would result in less proceeds at closing. This can also happen if the house falls in value. If your house would decline in value, creating less equity, you may have to pay off the home equity line and/or face a higher interest rate on the loan. You should never take home equity and invest in the market. This is a dangerous practice that encompasses too much risk.

2. Debt Management

If you are in the fortunate situation of having no debts, congratulations! If you come from the school of thought that you don't ever want to owe anything to anybody, debt management is not an issue. However, in today's society, this ideology is very uncommon and many people could use some strategies on effectively managing their debt.

Financially, it would make sense to rank all of your debts from highest to lowest interest, paying attention to the after-tax cost of borrowing. Since consumer debt is not tax-deductible, those rates are taken at face value. However, a mortgage or home equity loan is deductible, so the real rate of return is the after-tax cost.

To give another general rule of thumb, credit cards and consumer debt would be the first to pay off, if they have the highest interest rates. Then you would want to work away at the furniture loan, the used car loan, the new car loan, student loans, and finally, the home mortgage. Nowadays there are many credit cards that offer very low interest rates on balance transfers, which can be a temporary solution. But beware that the rate after the introductory period is not actually higher than your current card.

It is also important to look at debt management from a cash flow standpoint as well as an emotional standpoint. With this in mind, it can make sense to pay off a lower-interest loan if it will improve your cash flow dramatically, or if emotionally it is important for you to get it paid off for some other reason. Many people find a sense of satisfaction in paying debts off completely. Once one debt is paid off, take the extra cash and immediately begin paying off another loan more aggressively, so that cash does not get absorbed into the budget.

Check your credit report. It's a good idea to review your credit report every year. The financial information included in this report will have a bearing on whether you can obtain a loan, get auto or home insurance, rent an apartment, or even apply for a job. Contact the credit bureaus and correct any errors you find. I would suggest starting at www.annualcreditreport.com.

3. Risk Management

Protecting yourself against unforeseen catastrophic losses is the third critical area of the base of the pyramid and the *Security and Confidence Stage*. In fact, think of this as a three-legged stool. Kick one leg out, and the stool will not stand. The financial pyramid is just like that.

Important insurance coverage can include health and major medical, auto, disability, long-term care, and homeowners or renters. In many cases, life and/or disability insurance are overlooked. However, these can be very important depending on your personal situation.

The reason for placing risk management at this point is obvious. You need to protect yourself from losses that would create such a hole that you may otherwise never dig yourself out. Then, once you are on your way to financial independence, insurance plays an equally important role in protecting your assets.

While you don't want to have any gaps in your insurance protection, you certainly don't want to overlap or duplicate coverage. The ideal financial plan will have you paying reasonable premium levels while providing maximum protection. Remember, the major role of insurance is to protect against catastrophic losses. A common mistake is trying to insure too many contingencies or not using deductibles to your advantage.

You will want to ask yourself a couple of questions before purchasing insurance:

- Is the premium for this coverage going to dramatically affect my lifestyle?
- If I do not buy this coverage and suffer the losses that would have been covered, would I be in grave financial trouble?

If the answer to the first question is "No" and to the second "Yes," the insurance in question is right for you. If not, reconsider the structure and price of the insurance. Consult an experienced financial professional to help you determine the appropriate levels of coverage and how to structure your insurance within the context of a comprehensive financial plan.

When it comes to life insurance, it is easy to become confused. Some complicated terminology like "term life," "whole life," "universal life," and "variable whole life" may put you off, but by understanding just a few terms and some of the benefits and disadvantages, you will be much more prepared to evaluate the coverage that is best for you. If structured correctly, life insurance can be one of the most versatile and powerful financial tools available. Life insurance products contain fees, such as mortality and expense charges, and may contain restrictions, such as surrender charges.

- *Term Life:* While the premiums are low for the young, the price increases dramatically as you get older. Although young couples with children may find term life insurance to be the only affordable option, it is important to remember that this option brings no investment benefits. To optimize value on the policy, a guaranteed renewal clause allows for renewal to the policy without a medical requalification. Another value-adding option is a clause that allows a conversion from a renewable term policy to a permanent policy without proof of insurability.

- *Whole Life:* The most appealing feature of whole life insurance is its unchanging premium and guaranteed long-term coverage. Also, it builds up a tax-deferred "cash value." The cash value is what the insurer will return on cancellation of the policy. But whole life costs more than term life initially. Some critics believe whole life's cash value grows too slowly and, as an investment option, the buyer is better off buying term insurance and investing the difference in the stock market. The policies' rates of returns today are much more competitive than in the past, and this can be a very viable policy for a portion of your financial plan.

- *Adjustable/Universal Life:* The main feature of this policy is the flexibility in initial design and the ability to change as your needs change. If money gets tight, with this type of policy it's possible to lower the annual premium. You can also increase or decrease the death benefit as your needs change. Typically, increases in death benefit require additional proof of insurability.

- *Variable Life:* The cash values are invested into investment sub-accounts with your choice of the allocation to stocks, bonds, and/or money markets. The policy's cash value can increase if the investments do well. But the opposite could also occur. Look ahead to the next chapter for a more advanced discussion of this type of policy.

Disability insurance is one of the most important and overlooked types of insurance coverage. The odds of a long-term disability (lasting ninety days or longer) are 144 percent greater than death occurring during one's working years. (Source: www.disabilityquotes.com/Occupations/page2.cfm) And this is for the average person. While many employers provide group disability insurance, the benefits are generally 60 percent of one's income and taxable. The net effect is that only 40 to 45 percent of your income is protected.

Remember, you get what you pay for. Searching the Internet for the cheapest insurance policy often results in coverage that will not protect you and your family adequately. A competent insurance agent or financial planner can provide a valuable service, and should be used. They can be the best resource in helping you to select adequate coverage at appropriate prices, and at claim time they can help you decipher the paperwork. Choosing someone you trust, especially someone who comes recommended from a reliable source, will prove invaluable. Also, there may be some other aspects of your overall financial plan that, if reworked, can help you maximize your insurance protection, while building wealth for the future using better strategies than you were aware of.

As your assets grow, it is wise to expand your umbrella liability insurance coverage. The limits built into most homeowners and auto policies are minimal. This coverage actually protects your assets in the event that you or a family member cause harm due to your negligence. In addition, be sure to ask your agent for excess umbrella liability coverage for uninsured/underinsured motorists. This coverage protects you and your family for negligent acts caused by others.

In many cases, insurance is thought of as a "necessary evil." You have to have it, but it only benefits you if you have a claim. I look at the insurance coverage I own as a valuable part of an overall comprehensive financial plan. The peace of mind I have by knowing my family and I are covered is worth a lot. In addition, I can be more aggressive with my other savings and investments, because I know my risk management needs are taken care of.

Looking back to the Middle Ages, we get a glimpse of the importance of insurance. People of wealth built fabulous castles and filled them with treasures. They always devoted significant resources to protecting those assets in the form of an army, a moat, and so on. In a sense, that was an early form of an insurance policy. So as you continue to build your net worth, you should review and update your insurance to be sure you are maximizing your coverage and protecting you and your family and your wealth.

5

The Capital Accumulation Stage

This stage represents a large amount of assets you will build up over your lifetime. The assets that tend to comprise this stage are quite varied. Some of the investments include individual stocks and bonds, mutual funds, variable life insurance cash values, and equity in real estate or in a business. Aside from the equity you build into your retirement plan, the majority of your financial independence will come from these investments. While these assets can also serve as emergency reserves, the investment horizon is usually five years or longer.

Keep in mind that all investments have risk. However, there are varying degrees and types of risk. The risk most often associated with an investment involves a fluctuating principal or a sudden depreciation in the stock market, as in October 1987 or the bear markets of 2000–2002 and 2007–2009. A corporate bond or government security holds the risk of loss of principal due to an increase in interest rates. Even a relatively safe investment such as a money market fund has, in addition to market risk, purchasing power risk, because after taxes and inflation are figured in, your dollars could be worth less than when you originally invested. A summary of the types of risk is found towards the end of Chapter 3.

Saving money is one of the most important criteria in assuring financial success. Get in the habit now of saving between 10 and 20 percent of your gross income (10 percent if you are starting when you are in your mid-twenties, and 20 percent if you are over age forty). By living below your total income, even to this small degree, not only will your money be worth more in the long run by wisely investing it, but you will also cultivate a responsible attitude toward your money. Keeping up with the Joneses has become a national epidemic. But the real truth is that the millionaires next door don't concern themselves with flaunting their wealth, which explains why they are wealthy. Some of the financial ideas and products that belong in the *Capital Accumulation Stage* are discussed here.

Variable life policies are becoming increasingly popular. Because of their unique investment opportunities, their tax deferral potential, and their return potential, this new type of insurance policy should be examined by anyone who is investing money at the *Capital Accumulation Stage*. Such policies allow an individual to purchase a single financial instrument providing for both life insurance and long-term accumulation goals. Obviously, your level of insurance needs and wants has a large bearing on how the policy is structured, and it's important to carefully structure loans and withdrawals to avoid negative income tax results. Investments will fluctuate, and the cash values available for loans, withdrawals, or redemptions may be worth more or less than originally invested.

For many Americans, one of the most substantial forms of saving is simply making a monthly payment on your home. Generally speaking, real estate has long been a favorite investment tool for its tax benefits and as a buffer against inflation. Although there can be significant investment benefits in the long term, buying real estate is not without its risks. Deflation may decrease property values, or suspected long-term growth in a given area may not occur. Changes in tax law may reduce or eliminate anticipated tax benefits. Also, real estate is not liquid, so the necessity of a quick sale may require a substantial reduction in price.

The terms "stock" or "share" both refer to a partial ownership interest in a corporation, or equity. As a stockholder, you'll be able to vote for the company's board of directors, and receive information on the firm's activities and business results. You may share in "dividends" or current profits.

Investors typically buy and hold stock for its long-term growth potential. Stocks with a history of regular dividends are often held for both income and growth. As the long-term growth of a company cannot be predicted, the short-term market value of the company's stock will fluctuate up and down. If your financial need or your fear causes you to sell when the market is "down" (also called a "bear market"), a capital loss can result. If the market is "up" (also called a "bull market"), the investor can realize a capital gain when selling.

While stocks represent ownership in a business, bonds are debt issued by institutions such as the federal government, corporations, and state and local governments. At the bonds' "maturity," the principal amount will be returned. In the meantime, bondholders receive interest. When first issued, a bond will have a specified interest rate, or "yield." If a bond is traded on a public exchange, the market price will fluctuate, generally with changes in interest rates.

Using a mutual fund is an excellent way to lower your risk, because you are diversifying through a number of stocks. A properly designed mutual fund portfolio is generally the most appropriate method of accumulating wealth at this point in the financial pyramid. Some funds have higher market risk, meaning they can fluctuate quite dramatically. Past experience shows that funds that have the most risk have upside and downside potential that needs to be carefully considered. Funds with lower market risk often have inflation risk. These funds usually produce lower returns that may not keep up with inflation.

If your investment horizon is relatively short (up to five years), a more conservatively balanced fund, equity income fund, or even a medium-term corporate bond or government securities fund will likely be the most appropriate. When your investment horizon is longer, growth-oriented stock funds are generally going to be the best choice. Again, each circumstance is different, and the advice of a competent professional will be valuable. Most firms have a short investment attitude questionnaire you can answer to help you determine the appropriate asset allocation strategy that meets your needs.

Diversify! Diversify! Diversify! Nothing else will be as crucial to your portfolio as diversifying and having a long-term vision. It's important to diversity not only by asset class, but also by tax treatment and time horizon. We all know the proverb "Don't put all your eggs in one basket." Well, take it to the extreme— don't put all the baskets on the same truck, and don't drive all the trucks down the same road! It's not necessary to look too far back to recall the faddish investing in technology and start-up companies of the late 1990s. Too many investors lost significant wealth when the overvalued stocks plunged, and those eager investors expecting big returns were left with substantial losses.

Sometimes misunderstood, the main goal of diversification is not to maximize your return, but to minimize your risk and lower your volatility. The basic premise is that there is as much risk in being out of the market when it goes up as being in the market when it goes down, especially for your long-term money. As an example, take the period between 1926 and 1995, a period of 840 months. If you were out of the market during the thirty top-performing months—about 3.6 percent of the time—you would have ended up with a return similar to Treasury bills! While diversification does not guarantee against loss, it is a method used to manage risk.

Some additional strategies to employ when investing include dollar cost averaging and portfolio rebalancing. Dollar cost averaging is the process of investing a fixed amount of money each month (or quarter, or year) without worrying about whether the market is up or down. When it is down, you will buy more shares, bringing your average share price down. Over time, besides the element of forced savings, you will hopefully see returns you are happy with. Dollar cost averaging does not assure a profit, nor does it protect against loss in declining markets. This investment strategy requires regular investments regardless of the fluctuating price of the investment. You should consider your financial ability to continue investing through periods of low price levels.

When there is a large amount of money to invest, coming up with an investment policy and adhering to it is a must. Once an overall asset allocation mix is chosen based on your goals and objectives, stick to it and change only if there are significant changes in the economy, the portfolio, and/or your goals and objectives. Then, on a regular basis, either quarterly, semiannually, or annually, rebalance the portfolio back to the asset allocation you started with. With this strategy, your investment mix does not get skewed towards more or less risk and volatility. Many current portfolio managers have the capability of providing this rebalancing process on an automatic basis.

A well-balanced portfolio is properly diversified by the following asset decisions:

- Growth stocks: large, medium, and small[1]
- Value stocks: large, medium, and small
- International stocks: developed countries, emerging markets[2]
- Fixed income: corporate bonds, government bonds, high yield bonds
- Real estate: real property, low correlation with stocks[3]

There are many good resources to turn to that will help you take this process much further than the scope of this book. Some of those are found in Chapter 11. I think some of the best information can come from a competent and qualified financial advisor who will listen to you and develop a plan that meets your needs.

In general, a higher investment risk is best for those who:

- Can accept short-term losses
- Believe gains will offset losses over the long run
- Will not leave the investment if one or two bad years occur
- Have a long investment time horizon

The best way to learn sound market advice is to listen to the experts. The following quotes from mutual fund leaders all stress the futility of market timing:

---

[1] Investments in smaller company and micro-cap stocks generally carry a higher level of volatility and risk over the short term.
[2] Investment risks associated with international investing, in addition to other risks, include currency fluctuations, political and economic instability, and differences in accounting standards.
[3] Investment risks associated with investing in the real estate fund/portfolio, in addition to other risks, include rental income fluctuation, depreciation, property tax value changes, and differences in real estate market values.

Peter Lynch: *"My single-most important piece of investment advice is to ignore the short-term fluctuations of the market. From one year to the next, the stock market is a coin flip. It can go up or down. The real money in stocks is made in the third, fourth, and fifth year of your investments, because you are participating in a company's earnings, which grow over time."*

Warren Buffet: *"I do not have, never have had, and never will have an opinion where the stock market will be a year from now."*

Sir John Templeton: *"Ignore fluctuations. Do not try to outguess the stock market. Buy a quality portfolio, and invest for the long term."*

So, to drive it home, invest for the long term and be patient!

Variable life insurance, variable annuities, and mutual funds are sold only by prospectus. The prospectus contains important information about the product's charges and expenses, as well as the risks and other information associated with the product. You should carefully consider the risks and investment charges of a specific product before investing. You should always read the prospectus carefully before investing.

6

The Tax-Advantaged Stage

The focus of this stage is to try to significantly delay, reduce, and/or minimize the impact of taxes on your financial picture. Why? To accumulate and create the highest net worth you possibly can. One method of delaying the tax involves investing dollars into qualified retirement plans. This means the dollars are made on a before-tax (qualified) basis. Again, the taxes are not eliminated. They are just deferred until the funds are withdrawn. These plans include individual retirement accounts (IRAs), simplified employee pensions (SEPs), tax-sheltered annuities (TSAs), pension and profit-sharing plans, 401k plans, and so on.

The main advantage behind these plans is that the government has given you a significant motivation to save money because your taxable income is reduced dollar for dollar by the contribution, which will then save you anywhere from 10 to 35 percent of the deposit in taxes. In other words, your adjusted gross income is less, which means your taxable income is reduced. While these accounts are good places to defer and delay the tax liability during your working years, they present some problems at retirement because of the tax due then. And transferring qualified assets to heirs can present some tax nightmares if not handled carefully.

The general principal here is to save money into these plans when you are in a higher tax bracket, and withdraw the funds at retirement when you are in a lower tax bracket. I do see some problems, though. In some cases, when a person is early in their career and the income and tax bracket is low, it doesn't make any sense to put a lot of money into an IRA or 401k. Why defer money when you are in the lowest tax bracket you will ever be in? Instead, you may want to contribute to the 401k just up to where the employer matches those funds, but then again, only if you plan to be at that job for a few years to become vested (the employer's matching funds are yours if you are vested when you leave), and have taken care of the *Security and Confidence Stage* of your financial plan.

The reason the *Tax-Advantaged Stage* belongs above the *Capital Accumulation Stage* and *Security and Confidence Stage* of the pyramid is because the money deposited into these plans is normally not available until you reach the age of fifty-nine and a half. (There is a 10 percent IRS penalty for distributions taken within the first five years or prior to age fifty-nine and a half.) There are methods of getting your money out early by borrowing the funds or if disabled or have a hardship situation, but for the most part money flowing into these plans should be regarded as retirement money that cannot be touched until then.

Various Types of Retirement Plans

My intention here is not to give an in-depth description of every type of qualified plan available, but rather a brief description of each to help you understand basic terms and definitions associated with each different plan. Highlights of qualified plans include:

- Tax-deductible contributions
- Tax-deferred growth of investment earnings
- Most protected from claims of creditors

Some drawbacks of qualified plans include:

- Plan assets are generally illiquid until you reach age fifty-nine and a half. (10 percent IRS penalty applies to distributions prior to age fifty-nine and a half.)
- Annual contributions may be restrictive, in particular for the high-income medical specialist.
- All distributions are taxed at ordinary income.
- Complexity of plan design, setup, and administration can be high.

Here is a brief discussion of the various retirement plans.

Simple IRAs

A Simple IRA is generally a good option for a business with a small number of employees. A Simple IRA allows all employees to contribute a portion of their salary each paycheck, and will require that an employer contribution be made on behalf of all eligible employees. Current guidelines allow each employee to set aside up to $11,500 ($13,000 if age fifty or over) in 2009. Contributions made to the plan will be 100 percent tax-deductible. In addition, the employer or practice owner must *either* match employee contributions dollar for dollar up to 3 percent of an employee's compensation *or* make a contribution of 2 percent of compensation for all eligible employees, regardless of whether they are contributing their own money to the plan. Simple IRAs are easy to set up, very inexpensive to administer, and very attractive for smaller medical practices looking to offer a qualified retirement plan without a lot of cost or hassle.

401k Plans

With a 401k plan, employers may allow their employees to choose to defer up to $16,500 ($22,000 if age fifty or over) annually into the plan on a pre-tax basis. In addition, the employer may elect to contribute a portion into the individual employee's account. For example, suppose an employee earning $60,000 of annual income contributes the full 15 percent into the plan and the employer makes a 3 percent matching contribution. The total contribution made into the plan would be $10,800 ($9,000 plus 3 percent of $60,000, or $1,800).

The employer may place a vesting schedule on the matching contributions. You would be required to remain with the employer a certain number of years for the matching contribution to "vest." A summary of 401k plan benefits include:

- High contribution limits for employer and employees
- A competitive plan to attract and retain key people
- Loan provisions for hardships and emergencies
- Flexibility with respect to matching contributions

Safe Harbor 401k Plans

A safe harbor 401k plan is intended to encourage plan participation among all employees and ease the administrative burden by eliminating IRS tests normally required with a traditional 401k plan. A safe harbor 401k plan allows employees to contribute a percentage of their pay into the plan. It then *requires* an employer contribution on behalf of all eligible employees, whether they are participating in the plan or not. This contribution is also always immediately vested. While there are several permitted matching formulas, an example would be 100 percent of participant contributions up to 3 percent of pay, plus an additional 50 percent of participant contributions up to the next 2 percent of pay.

Roth 401k

A Roth 401k is a new type of retirement plan that combines the tax treatment of a Roth IRA with annual contribution limits of a traditional 401k. You may opt to take advantage of the Roth 401k if currently in a lower tax environment today than you likely will be in retirement. Such a plan allows you to contribute up to $16,500 for 2009 on an after-tax basis. In other words, there is no tax benefit today associated with the contributions. However, the plan assets grow 100 percent tax-deferred and, provided certain requirements are met, all plan assets are withdrawn on a tax-free basis after age fifty-nine and a half.

Profit-Sharing Plans

Profit-sharing plans are designed to allow the employer to contribute to the plan on a discretionary basis. Depending on the terms of the plan, there is no set amount an employer needs to contribute each year. If contributions are made, you must have a set formula for determining how the contributions are allocated among all eligible plan participants. The maximum deductible contribution that can be made to a profit-sharing plan is 25 percent of eligible compensation, to a maximum of $49,000 in 2009. Eligible compensation is all the compensation an employer pays to eligible plan participants during the employer's tax year. Contributions are tax-deductible, and earnings accumulate on a tax-deferred basis. The employer takes the deduction for this contribution. The employer's contribution to each employee's account is not considered taxable income to the employees for the contribution year.

With a profit-sharing plan, the main benefit to the business owner is the flexible nature of the contributions. It is possible to adjust contributions each year, depending on profitability of the business, as long as contributions are frequent and ongoing. A real, tangible benefit of a profit-sharing plan for the employee is having contributions to the plan tied to the performance and overall profitability of the business.

Money Purchase Plans

A money purchase plan is very similar to a profit-sharing plan in terms of contribution limits, benefits to employer and employee, setup and ongoing administrative costs, and eligibility. The primary difference is that employer contribution is a plan requirement. This amount is stated in the plan document. The benefit of a money purchase plan for the employer is that the fixed annual contributions to the plan make it easier to budget for and offers a measure of comfort and predictability for the employee. The inflexibility is often a big enough drawback that most businesses gravitate to the other choices. It is beyond the scope of this text, but for certain situations (i.e., a small number of employees with one or two older and highly paid specialists), a money purchase plan and/or a variation of it can provide for sizable annual deferral limits that exceed the other plans.

Simplified Employee Pensions (SEP IRAs)

An SEP IRA is a retirement plan that looks much like a profit-sharing plan. The contribution limit is 25 percent of employee compensation up to a maximum of $49,000 in 2009. The administrative costs associated with an SEP IRA are very minimal, as are reporting and tax filing requirements. The plan must cover all employees who have worked for the group in three of the past five years and are twenty-one years or older. SEP IRA plans are attractive for medical groups that have unpredictable cash flow, as contributions to the plan can vary or not be made at all, depending on profitability. The contributions are 100 percent employer-paid with no employee contributions allowed.

SEP IRAs can also be particularly attractive for someone who has a small side business that is run from their home. Contributions for self-employment income are based on net income, minus 50 percent of self-employment taxes paid and any deductible plan contributions or a maximum of $49,000. Since self-employment income is taxed very heavily, such a plan can be a very effective tool to lessen the tax burden. In addition, SEP plans provide creditor protection at both the federal and state level.

In summary, qualified plans are an integral part of your retirement, and there are many ways you can design a plan. When your income is at the highest tax bracket, we generally advocate taking full advantage of the plan available to you through your employer and contributing the maximum annual contribution limit allowable under current tax law. If you have just started work and have questions or concerns regarding the existing plan or a new plan, I encourage you to contact a competent financial advisor for several reasons:

- Your qualified plan will likely be your largest retirement asset, and as such should be carefully invested and monitored.
- Tax laws surrounding such plans have changed considerably and continue to change each year. This requires more time on your part to ensure that you have the most appropriate plan that provides you maximum benefit given your circumstances.
- Tax arbitrage planning opportunities exist. You should invest in a qualified plan at a high tax bracket and withdraw the funds at a lower bracket. So your retirement income will likely come from several sources as you design a retirement income strategy to maximize your after-tax income.

Calculating Your Tax Bracket

Just for you, I have taken the 10,000-page tax code and narrowed it down to two pages (see pages 53 and 54). Wouldn't that be nice if preparing our taxes was that easy! This is, of course, a basic guide only, just for education purposes, and doesn't factor in some of the specifics such as childcare, student loan interest deductions, moving expenses, and so on. But surprisingly, this is fairly accurate in estimating the federal tax liability.

I encourage working with your accountant, running one of the tax software packages, or simply using this guide any time you have a major change in your life that will affect your taxes. Family changes such as a birth, death, or marriage all affect the tax you owe. Financial changes such as a new job, a raise, going back to school, or buying or moving to a new house will also impact your tax liability, and a new calculation should be made. Compare your calculation to the amount you are having withheld from your paycheck, and if you are withholding too much, change this with your employer by filling out a new W-4 form.

This is especially useful for a student graduating in May or June and starting employment mid-year. If you don't work with your employer on the correct tax withholding, they will take out an amount that would correspond to you working for the whole year. Generally, there are many expenses, and having a higher take-home pay would most likely be more beneficial than getting a tax refund the following spring.

There are some important basic points to understand about taxes. First, getting a large refund isn't really all that smart. It means you just gave the government an interest-free loan for the year. If you are a terrible saver and use this as a forced savings plan, I'm guessing it still backfires on you because you know the lump-sum tax refund is coming and you have plans for spending that amount too! In any event, I suggest that you estimate your tax liability in advance and try to end up about even. That avoids any under-withholding penalties and any unexpected tax liability due that you may not be prepared for.

The second point is that it is always in your best interest to make more money. I've heard people say, "I just got a raise (or a bonus, or whatever), and it jumped me into the next tax bracket, so I'm going to take home less!" That's not how it works. The tax system is a progressive tax, and the more income you make, the more you take home. It's just that each additional dollar is taxed at a higher percentage, but the first dollars are taxed the same. Repeated, moving into a higher tax bracket affects the last of your dollars you earn, but the first dollars are still taxed at the same rate.

As an example, let's look at the Basic Federal Tax Estimator on the next page. Plug in your income (wages, interest income, etc.), and subtract contributions to pre-tax accounts to get your adjusted gross income. From that, you subtract your personal exemptions and either the standard deduction or your itemized deductions, whichever is higher. Then look up your tax bracket on the chart. The tax bracket is the tax on each additional dollar you earn, or the tax that is saved by virtue of reducing your taxable income by a dollar.

Suppose you are single and your taxable income happens to be exactly $82,250. Your best friend's taxable income comes in at $82,251, or $1 more. Bummer for them, right? Yes and no. Their tax liability is only 28 cents more than yours, because each new dollar is taxed at the 28 percent rate. They still have a take-home pay of 72 cents more than you, so while at a higher tax bracket, their take-home pay is more. The total tax is calculated as follows:

First $8,350 of taxable income:	$835 ($8,350 × 0.10)
Next $25,600 of taxable income:	$3,840 ($25,600 × 0.15)
Next $48,300 of taxable income:	$12,075 ($48,300 × 0.25)
Total tax:	$16,750

Your friend's tax bill would be calculated the same as yours with another 28 of tax liability on the $1 above $82,250 at the 28 percent tax bracket. Work through your own situation a few times, and this should be easier to understand.

Basic Federal Tax Estimator

This is a guide only, and is current as of 2009. For the most current tax law information, see www.basictaxestimator.com. This does not factor in childcare, student loan interest deductions, medical expenses, moving, and so on.

Gross Income (Wages, interest income, etc.) $_____

Minus: **Adjustments** (IRA, 401k, TSA, etc.) $_____

Equals: **Adjusted Gross Income** $_____

Minus: **Personal Exemptions** ($3,650 × # in household) $_____
(Phased out as income exceeds certain limits)

And the higher of:

Standard Deduction (Single: $5,700; Married: $11,400) $_____

Or

Itemized Deductions $_____

      ☐   State Income Tax
      ☐   Home Mortgage Interest and Property Tax
      ☐   Charitable Contributions

Equals: **Taxable Income** $_____

Federal Income Tax Due (See tax table below): $_____

2009 Individual Income Tax Rates

Single	Married Filing Jointly
$0 to $8,350: 10%	$0 to $16,700: 10%
$8,351 to $33,950: 15%	$16,701 to $67,900: 15%
$33,951 to $82,250: 25%	$67,901 to $137,050: 25%
$82,251 to $171,550: 28%	$137,051 to $208,850: 28%
$171,551 to $372,950: 33%	$208,851 to $372,950: 33%
$372,951+: 35%	$372,951+: 35%

There are substantial tax benefits with a variety of non-qualified investments also. The term "non-qualified" means there is no immediate tax deduction when contributing to these accounts, but the tax benefits can be more beneficial over your lifetime. The following assets are generally part of the *Capital Accumulation Stage*, but I'll provide the discussion of the tax reduction strategy of each technique in this chapter.

Stocks

As stocks appreciate in value (for this discussion, we'll assume they appreciate) there is no tax due on the appreciation until the stock is sold. Along the way, if any dividends are paid, the tax rate is less (15 percent for the highest tax bracket) than the ordinary income tax rate. In addition, when the stock is sold, if held for over a year, the gain is taxed at the lower 15 percent capital gain rate. So there is a benefit of tax deferral during the holding period and tax minimizing due to the gain being treated as a capital gain.

Roth IRAs

Assuming you have all of your *Security and Confidence Stage* issues taken care of, and your income is such that you can use Roth IRAs, I would recommend it. You do not get a current tax deduction, but under current law, all the growth (again, assuming it grows) is tax-deferred. Then, when you take the money out of the Roth IRA at retirement, you receive it income tax-free. Would you rather pay tax on the seeds going into the ground, or the end-of-year harvest? Growth in a Roth IRA may not be withdrawn until the later of reaching age fifty-nine and a half or maintaining your Roth IRA for a period of five years. Withdrawals prior to this (or if not held for five years) are subject to a 10 percent early withdrawal penalty.

Real Estate

Real estate can be an excellent method of building wealth. Getting away from rent and into your first home is one obvious way. Another is leveraging the equity you have in your existing real estate into additional property. The growth is tax-deferred, and there are some favorable strategies available upon the sale and/or disposition. As for financing your house, contrary to popular belief, it can make sense to put little money down and stretch the mortgage out (and the tax deduction) in favor of freeing up cash flow for other goals and objectives.

Life Insurance

In addition to the death benefit, the benefits of a life insurance policy are much like those of the Roth IRA, with some additional features. As an accumulation tool, there is a cost for the insurance, so this is appropriate for someone who is younger and in good health and has a longer investment time horizon. The cash values grow tax-deferred and can be accessed income tax-free, if structured properly. It is generally best to avoid having the policy become a modified endowment policy. This occurs when too much money is contributed to a policy, and many favorable tax benefits are lost. Working with a very knowledgeable insurance or financial professional is a must if you are considering a policy as described here.

Having a permanent life insurance policy can help you maximize your overall net worth in some other ways too. You reduce your need for term insurance, which frees up cash. In fact, the most beneficial time to have a permanent life insurance policy in place is at retirement because of all the advantages it provides. Briefly, you can be more aggressive in using and enjoying your other assets, because the life insurance essentially provides a "permission slip" to do so. Work with your financial advisor to coordinate this with your overall financial plan.

State-Sponsored 529 College Plans

There are a number of methods of putting investments in your children's or grandchildren's names. If the funds are ultimately to help them with their future college education expenses, a 529 Plan may be the answer. Some states allow a state tax deduction on the contributions, and all of the plans grow tax-deferred. If the funds are withdrawn for tuition, room and board, and "qualifying" education needs, the funds can be withdrawn tax-free also. These funds can even be transferred between family members. For a lengthier discussion, as well as a link to your state-sponsored plan, go to www.savingforcollege.com. However, make sure your own financial security is assured and your financial pyramid is sound before aggressively putting money into your children's accounts.

Annuities

An annuity is marketed by an insurance company as their answer to other investments. There are numerous benefits of non-qualified annuities as another financial instrument. Namely, they grow tax-deferred, and for variable annuities you can switch between the separate accounts in a variable annuity without current income tax implications, and there are some death benefit guarantees to protect the value for your heirs. Withdrawals from annuities prior to age fifty-nine and a half are subject to a 10 percent early withdrawal penalty, as well as potential deferred sales charges. You also will want to review the asset protection laws of your state to see if annuities are protected. They are in numerous states, thus increasing their attractiveness as an investment.

Variable life insurance, variable annuities, and mutual funds are sold only by prospectus. The prospectus contains important information about the product's charges and expenses, as well as the risks and other information associated with the product. You should carefully consider the risks and investment charges of a specific product before investing. You should always read the prospectus carefully before investing.

An annuity is a long-term, tax-deferred investment vehicle designed for retirement. If the annuity will fund an IRA or other tax-qualified plan, the tax deferral feature offers no additional value. They are not FDIC/NCUA insured, bank guaranteed, or insured by any federal government agency. Variable annuities have additional expenses such as mortality and expense risk, administrative charges, investment management fees, and rider fees. Variable annuities are subject to market fluctuation, investment risk, and loss of principal. The guarantees of a variable annuity are based on the claims-paying ability of the issuing life insurance company. The guarantees and the claims-paying ability do not have any bearing on the performance of the investment options within a variable annuity.

What percentage exposure you have to each type of asset category will depend on your time horizon, risk profile, and overall objectives. Once your allocation is established, regular monitoring and periodic rebalancing will be critical in accomplishing the two most important objectives: lower levels of short-term volatility and the highest possible long-term rate of return.

What Do You Do At Retirement?

Estimating your retirement needs is an important factor to consider at this stage of the pyramid. A financial planning rule of thumb is to figure on needing 70 to 80 percent of your pre-retirement income, although more people are enjoying a retirement lifestyle that is close to their working years. This figure should be based on the income you plan to be earning at retirement, not that which you're making today. To estimate this, look at your current expenses and subtract the expenses and savings that will not be needed at retirement, and add in extra expenses (travel, medical, etc.) that may be needed then. Consider the following:

- Will you still be paying a mortgage?
- Do you anticipate hefty medical expenses for yourself or your spouse?
- Do you wish to travel extensively?
- Will your day-to-day living expenses be similar to, or less than, what they are now?

If your budget allows, and you have your *Security and Confidence Stage* taken care of, take full advantage of any 401k or similar plans your employer offers, at least up until the amount the employer matches. This type of retirement investment defers tax payment on the contributed earnings until the money is withdrawn, usually at retirement. If your employer matches any of your contribution, this is an added tax benefit.

If you are self-employed, consider an SEP or Simple IRA retirement plan, which also allows you to take advantage of the pre-tax growth that has been described in this chapter. Deciding on the correct retirement plan will be something a competent financial advisor can help you with.

Universal Retirement Truths

Over the years, as retirement planning has become increasingly complicated, there are four simple truths behind any advice we offer on retirement planning, no matter how complicated the specific issue.

Start Early

The sooner you begin contributing to your retirement plan, the more time your money has to compound. You can always make adjustments to keep your investment allocation on track with your risk tolerance and time horizon profile. However, if you delay getting started entirely, it is very difficult to catch up.

Diversify

With regard to your retirement plan, after you have determined an appropriate investment allocation for your contributions, make sure you understand the investment objectives of each individual fund you are investing in.

Two funds with different names may have very similar investment objectives as well as holdings. Deferring into each fund will not give you the same degree of diversification as investing in two funds with different objectives.

We recommend you work with a financial professional to determine an appropriate asset allocation for your retirement assets and make sure you achieve a high level of diversification among the investment options.

Invest Consistently

Most plans allow for contributions to be made on a payroll deduction basis. This allows for contributions to be made to your investments every month. This eliminates any tendency to "time" the market and put larger contributions at the optimal share price. Regular investing over time is a proven method that "forces" you to buy more shares when the price of a fund is down, and fewer when prices are higher.

The goal of dollar cost averaging is to produce a lower average cost per share over time.

Hang Tough

If your retirement is still fifteen, twenty, even thirty years away, it is appropriate (even crucial) to construct a more aggressive investment allocation than that of an investment objective with a shorter time horizon. It is perfectly natural that such an investment allocation will experience higher levels of short-term fluctuation. This is necessary to potentially achieve a higher long-term rate of return.

As the time when you will begin drawing on this money draws nearer, it will be necessary to begin shifting a greater percentage of your assets towards investments geared more towards capital preservation. The time to worry about this is not during your peak earning years when retirement is still many years away. Ideally, at retirement, you have multiple income sources and are withdrawing money from your qualified plans to "fill up" your 15 percent bracket, and supplementing that with withdrawals from your non-qualified funds, Roth IRAs, and variable life policies for maximum tax leverage and efficiency. This is an area where the advice and wisdom of an experienced financial planner will be very valuable.

7

529 College Savings Plans

When it comes to planning for your children's future education costs, the 529 College Savings Plans have been designed specifically for this financial goal. From an investment standpoint, such plans enjoy tax-deferred growth of earnings, extremely generous contribution limits, and currently tax-free distributions of investment gains for all qualified education expenses. (I'll expand on qualified expenses in a moment.)

My opinion is that the features that make such plans so attractive have less to do with their tax treatment and more to do with issues of control and flexibility.

Let's look at these plans from two difference perspectives:

- Investment and tax features
- Control and flexibility features

Tax and Investment Features

One frustrating aspect of investment planning from a tax perspective is that, when income increases beyond certain annual amounts, many investments that have attractive tax treatment become unavailable (Roth IRAs) or annual contribution limits become more restrictive as income goes up (401k plans). Neither of these is an issue with the 529 Plan. All investment earnings on the plan grow 100 percent tax-deferred, and the contribution limits are such that they would rarely be restrictive for the purpose of funding a child's education.

Contributions

Contributions to 529 Plans are not federally[4] tax-deductible, but are considered gifts for federal and estate tax purposes. Anyone may take advantage of the annual gift tax exclusion by contributing, as of 2009, $13,000 per year ($26,000 for married couples) to any beneficiary. There is also a very unique rule for 529 Plans that allows for an individual to utilize five years worth of annual gift tax exclusion for the named beneficiary by contributing up to $65,000 ($130,000 for married couples) in one calendar year.

The limits imposed on 529 Plans are, generally speaking, so high that it is difficult to envision a scenario where it would become restrictive. The total limits outside of the above-discussed annual limits do vary a bit from state to state. Provided you get started early on planning for your children's or grandchildren's future education costs to take full advantage of the tax-deferred growth of investment earnings, such limits should not present a problem.

Distributions

Money has been contributed to a 529 Plan for the benefit of a child or grandchild, and the plan balance has grown significantly over the years. Now it is time to begin withdrawing the money to pay for college expenses, so what happens? When money is withdrawn from the account, it will be considered one of two things: a qualified distribution or a non-qualified distribution.

- Distributions that are utilized to pay for qualified expenses such as room, board, tuition, and certain other expenses will be considered qualified withdrawals, and as such are free of both federal and, currently, state income tax. For the parent with a long time horizon and children bound for academic greatness (and the accompanying

---

[4] It should be noted that with many state plans there is a tax deduction for contributions to the state plan where you hold your primary residence. Because each state varies and the laws are changing, consult with a financial advisor who is familiar with the rules in your state.

price tag), there is potential to build up and withdraw all investment gains free of tax.

- Distributions that are utilized for anything other than a qualified expense will be considered a non-qualified distribution. The investment earnings will be taxed as ordinary income for the beneficiary and subject to a 10 percent penalty.

Control and Flexibility Features

The tax and investment features of 529 Plans are undeniably attractive and make such plans a very powerful financial tool for parents and grandparents who want to help with future educational needs. However, given the uncertainty of a young child's academic future, I often find reluctance among my clients to fund such vehicles for their child, who may or may not need the money. These uncertainties are very well addressed in 529 Plans.

Let's look at some of their benefits from a control and flexibility standpoint.

Who controls the account? The account owner controls the account. If your child reaches the age of majority in your home state, the 529 Plan balance does not become an asset of your child. You, as account owner, control how and when distributions are to be made.

Who can contribute to the account? Anyone may make contributions to the plan.

What happens if my child receives a scholarship or goes to a less expensive school? Perhaps one of the most attractive features of 529 Plans from a flexibility standpoint is the ability to change beneficiaries at any point. However, to avoid triggering penalty on investment earnings, the new beneficiary must be a family member of the previous beneficiary. The ability to move money in one designated 529 Plan to another child's plan, should he or she not go to school, attend a less expensive school, receive a scholarship, or any other reason, is a unique feature that gives parents a great deal of flexibility.

What happens if money is not used for college? If the money being withdrawn from a 529 Plan is being used for anything other than a qualified higher education expense, the investment earnings will be taxed at the beneficiaries' tax rate, plus a 10 percent penalty on earnings. Pulling money out of 529 Plans for non-qualified expenses should be avoided.

Must the beneficiary go to school in the state whose plan I used? No. Currently, all states recognize other state-sponsored 529 Plans, and as such, all distributions for qualified expenses will be both federally and state tax-exempt.

Funding Your Child's 529 College Savings Plan

With all the advantages of 529 Plans, the obvious question becomes, "How do we fund a plan for our child?"

When determining how to take full advantage of such plans, there are several assumptions you can predict with a fairly high degree of accuracy. Such factors include:

- Year in which your child enters college
- How many years (four or five) of post-secondary education you wish to be able to fund
- The average inflation-adjusted cost for both public and private education costs
- The percentage of the total cost you as a parent wish to be able to pay for

There are also many more variables you must simply make a best estimate for. A few of these factors include:

- The rate of inflation for college costs. College costs have experienced significant levels of increase over the years, and will likely continue to rise at a greater rate than the overall cost of living.
- The investment rate of return of the assets in the 529 Plan
- Where your child will attend school

All of these variables must be considered when determining how to fund your child's plan to arrive at the most important objective: having adequate funds available within the plan to be able to pay for the type of education, the length of education, and the location of the education you planned for. Any outcome other than this will result in one of two scenarios:

- *Not enough money saved up in the 529 Plan.* This will likely result in funds being withdrawn from other investment vehicles that have not grown tax-deferred and will likely not enjoy the tax benefits when withdrawn. As qualified distributions will be both state and federally tax-exempt, investment gains from other sources will likely be subject to tax. As discussed earlier, this is where an over-funded variable life insurance policy can come in very handy.

- *Too much money saved up in the 529 Plan.* The likely result of too much money in the plan will be excessive non-qualified distributions. While the earnings will be taxed at your child's rate and thus at a lower rate, this is only in the event that it is withdrawn for the benefit of the beneficiary. Should the money *not* be withdrawn for the benefit of your child, all investment earnings will taxed at *your* ordinary income rate plus a 10 percent penalty. So err on the conservative side and fund a 529 Plan at a level you feel comfortable with.

My conclusion is that 529 College Savings Plans are excellent financial tools for the purpose of saving for future college costs. Like all aspects of your financial planning, regular monitoring is critical. As your child's academic greatness (hopefully!) begins to materialize, adjusting the contributions to the plan accordingly will ensure that the many benefits can be maximized.

A 529 Plan is a tax-advantaged investment program designed to help pay for qualified education costs. Participation in a 529 Plan does not guarantee that the contributions and investment returns will be adequate to cover higher education expenses. Contributors to the plan assume all investment risk, including the potential for loss of principal and any penalties for non-educational withdrawals.

Your state of residence may offer state tax advantages to residents who participate in the in-state plan. You may miss out on certain state tax advantages, should you choose another state's 529 Plan. Any state-based benefits should be one of many appropriately weighted factors to be considered in making an investment decision. You should consult your financial, tax, or other advisor to learn more about how state-based benefits (including any limitations) would apply to your specific circumstances. You may also wish to contact your home state's 529 Plan program administrator to learn more about the benefits that might be available to you by investing in the in-state plan.

8

The Speculation Stage

The Speculation Stage involves risking money you can afford to lose. Some people are never comfortable with this and thus should not consider it. These people should simply build their financial pyramid wider. This stage can involve different things for different people. It might mean investing into a small business you're starting or investing in a friend's business. It could be buying very speculative individual stocks or aggressive specialty mutual funds.

Subjecting your money where the principal has a high degree of volatility and risk has potentially high returns, but your money could also be lost completely. It is appropriate that this stage fits at the top of the pyramid, because if the money is lost, it won't be devastating to your overall financial plan.

My rule of thumb when deciding how much to risk in a business opportunity or other aggressive venture.is one year's worth of net worth growth. Never invest more than this! In a worst case scenario, if you lost the entire amount of your investment, you have basically lost one year's worth of financial progress. While not fun, it is not financially devastating. People get into trouble and can't recover financially when they take a lifetime's worth of savings and gamble with it.

As an example, let's say that your net worth is $100,000, and conservatively projected a year from now, it will be $110,000. This growth could be from additional savings, reducing debts, and/or growth from your existing assets. In any event, the $10,000 projected growth is the amount that could be considered for a very speculative investment.

In the event that an opportunity has come along that requires more than this amount, do not be tempted to risk more. Consider lowering your investment, delaying the timing until your net worth has grown, or involving a financial partner. The following ideas are just a few examples of possibilities that exist:

- Buying individual stocks of new companies
- Buying stock in initial public offerings
- Buying stock on margin (Be very careful!)
- Investing in a friend's or family member's new business
- Buying raw land and/or real estate for speculation
- Trading commodities (Be careful here!)

Again, keep in mind that speculative investments, while valid financial tools, are typically used only by extremely savvy investors and/or high net worth investors and institutions. They are not recommended to anyone who cannot afford to lose a substantial amount of their net worth. These investments carry an extraordinary amount of risk, and generally require intensive research and knowledge to carry out the investment.

In summary, no one has ever gotten into trouble financially by being too conservative for too long. Sure, there are some potential lost opportunity costs, but you can get into a lot of financial trouble by being too aggressive with too much money. That's why the financial pyramid is such a useful tool to help organize and prioritize these decisions.

You've worked hard to educate yourself in your field. I hope this book provides you with a framework to begin your financial plan, and that you achieve all of your goals and dreams.

9

Frequently Asked Questions

Security and Confidence

1. *How much money should I have in emergency reserves?* As a general rule of thumb, you should have three to six months worth of income easily available as emergency reserves. This doesn't necessarily have to be in a savings account. In fact, I currently have an approved line of credit against the equity of our home, and use that as my emergency reserve, minimizing my need to keep money in low-yielding accounts. However, as mentioned before, there are risks associated with home equity loans.

2. *In which order and how should I go about paying off my debts?* Normally you'll want to pay off the highest after-tax interest loans to the lowest. It's important to consider the after-tax rate, because certain loans are tax-deductible while others are not. For example, the interest on your mortgage and student loan is usually deductible, but the interest on your car loan or credit card usually is not. Also take into consideration the total amount of the loan. If one low-interest loan has a relatively low balance, but you would feel much better to get it out of your mind, then by all means pay it off.

3. *Which is the right type of life insurance, and how much do I need?* Unfortunately, this is not an easy question to answer simply. Generally you'll want to have at least eight times your income and ideally up to fifteen times your income (human life value) in life insurance. A trusted insurance agent or financial planner can be a valuable resource in deciphering the many options that meet your needs, and mesh with your overall financial plan.

4. *What are the most common financial mistakes people make?*

- Having their long-term money invested too conservatively
- Having their short-term money invested too aggressively
- Not planning for emergencies or potential losses
- Not planning for the future of their family business
- Not taking the time to plan
- Not seeking out the help of a qualified advisor

5. *How can I appropriately measure my financial success?* Regularly updating your net worth statement will be an ideal way to gauge your financial progress.

6. *When should I start saving and investing?* This is one of the few black and white answers in planning for your financial future. If you haven't started already, then the only correct response is *today!*

Capital Accumulation

1. *From a financial standpoint, is it better to buy or lease a car?* Like so many issues dealt with in this book, the answer here also depends on individual circumstances. When considering these two options, ask yourself the following questions:

- Do I need the security of low mileage and a warranty at all times?
- Do I plan to upgrade my vehicle every few years?
- Do I have the financial security to always make monthly car payments?
- Do I prefer the hassle of shopping for a new car periodically over that of having occasional breakdowns?

If you answered "Yes" to these questions, leasing may be the best option for you. However, if you would rather keep your car until the repair costs outweigh the cost of a monthly car payment, then buying a car outright makes more sense.

2. What is a sales load on a mutual fund, class A share? There are several fees that should be understood when making a mutual fund purchase with A shares:

- *Up-Front Sales Load:* This cost takes on a greater significance the shorter time the fund is held. This is an up-front fee or commission to be used for compensation for the broker or financial planner or adviser. When doing your own research without the help of a third party, you may be more inclined to use a fund that does not have an up-front sales load. If you are using a financial advisor, there is no problem with paying an up-front sales load if:

    a. You know how much the commission is (he/she should let you know).
    b. The amount you're paying is buying you worthwhile advice and saving you time.

- *Management Fee:* This is the annual expense built into an investment. All funds have a management fee. Be sure you ask what the fee is and what that buys you in terms of service and value.

3. What should I consider when buying a home?

- Consider purchasing a home valued at no more than triple your gross annual income. It is to your advantage to minimize the number of real estate transactions you engage in during your lifetime, because they involve substantial fees, commissions, and transaction costs. Rather than getting a smaller "starter" home, requiring an upgrade in three to five years, try to stretch yourself a bit, especially when interest rates are lower and the housing market is favorable.

- Be sure to have an attorney involved in the purchase. Because this is such an important financial commitment, a lawyer should look over the offer, closing statements, and other documents. The money you spend for an attorney will be well worth the peace of mind it brings.

- When financing, compare loan options as aggressively as you looked for your house. There are many differences among financial institutions in transaction fees, costs, and interest rates charged.

- In securing a loan, consider putting down as small a down payment as the bank will allow, and use a thirty-year mortgage. Consider using a fixed rate if you plan to be in the house seven years or longer. Consider an adjustable rate if you plan to stay in the house less than seven years. Keep in mind that if you have a 6 percent mortgage, the real cost to you would be approximately 4.3 percent, because you can deduct the interest. (Assuming you are in a 28 percent marginal tax bracket and you can earn an after-tax rate of return of 4.4 percent or better. Your net worth will grow faster by investing that money elsewhere.)

- Try to avoid private mortgage insurance with a combination of two loans, if possible. One loan is the traditional mortgage, and the other is held by the bank as a home equity line of credit at interest only.

- Other methods of preserving a good cash flow and keeping the up-front costs to a minimum include making an offer subject to the seller paying some of the closing costs, including appliances in the offer, and so on. A good realtor and lawyer can be creative with this, depending upon the circumstances of the sale.

- Unless you use a buyer's broker, the real estate agent represents the *seller* in the transaction. They will work their hardest to find a place you are satisfied with, but ultimately have a fiduciary responsibility to obtain the highest price they can for the seller.

4. What's the best way to save for my child's college education? There are many options available, and doing some research will be necessary in order to find out which will work best for you. A 529 plan is my favorite option and has tax advantages that vary according to state. To find out more, check www.savingforcollege.com.

General

1. How do I make some tough decisions about my finances? First of all, if a decision is hard to make, then either the timing isn't right or you don't have enough facts. So I suggest to keep researching and asking questions until you feel more comfortable with the decision.

2. *Do you have any advice for couples?* I think all couples should respect each other's opinions on a financial subject. If they are at odds, it may be because one person is thinking about the decision from the financial perspective and the other is looking at it from the emotional standpoint. Listen to each other, and try to find the common ground. Also, consider establishing a dollar limit on decisions that must be made together and in agreement. For instance, if a financial purchase or decision is something that would cost $250 or more, both people must agree on the decision.

10

Case Studies

Observations and Overview

In this chapter, we provide four specific case studies that demonstrate the concepts outlined in this book. These will show that the pyramid of financial needs can be used in most circumstances as a method of organizing and prioritizing financial decisions. Of course, much of this is subjective, and ultimately the correct answer merges the quantitative and qualitative aspects of the decision into a financial plan you are comfortable with. We hope you find the following case studies to be a very helpful addition to the understanding of the techniques presented earlier in this book.

The following case studies are fictitious, and any similarities to any actual person(s) or situation(s) are coincidental.

Case Study #1: Recent College Graduate

Jillian is twenty-four and graduated with her engineering degree two years ago. She recently accepted a new position with a nationally known company doing software design. There is great potential within this firm, and she sees management opportunities in the future. She is in a serious relationship, but she always wants to maintain her financial independence. The past couple of years have been really challenging for Jillian, as her father passed away from lung cancer last year and her family was not prepared for it financially. With everything that was going on with her family, she accumulated some credit card debt and used up most of her savings. She wants to get back on track for the future.

Her primary financial goals at this time are to:

- Start saving to buy a condo or house in a few years
- Pay off her credit card
- Build her savings back up
- Keep saving for retirement
- Not become a burden on her family should something happen to her

The Numbers

Jillian's annual salary is now $55,000 in her current position with ABC Inc., but she expects it to continue to increase to $90,000 within the next five years. She contributes 10% of her salary to her 401k. They match this dollar for dollar up to the first 6% of income contributed, and she participates in the employee stock ownership plan at 5% of her income, where she can purchase company stock at a 15% discount. ABC Inc. provides Jillian with long-term disability insurance, covering up to 50% of her salary, at no cost to her. She currently has a roommate, which cuts her expenses in half. She is frugal, and she currently has $1,000 savable each month to put towards her goals.

Net Worth Statement

Fixed Assets:
      Checking Account: $2,000
      Savings Account (at 1.5%): $2,000
      Total Fixed Assets: **$4,000**

Variable Assets:
      Current 401k: $760
      Old 401k: $7,000
      Employee Stock Ownership Plan: $500
      Total Variable Assets: **$8,260**

Personal and Other Assets:
      Vehicle: $10,000
      Personal Property: $2,000
      Total: **$12,000**

Total Assets: **$24,260**

Liabilities:
      Vehicle Loan (6.75%): $8,000
      Credit Cards (10%): $3,000
      Student Loans (3.75%): $15,000
      Total Liabilities: **$26,000**

Net Worth (Assets Minus Liabilities):   **−$1,740**

The Financial Plan

Security and Confidence Stage:

- Open an interest rate-sensitive money market mutual fund to use as her emergency reserve. This account will pay her more than her current savings with the credit union. Fund at a level of $250 per month. This will provide her with that safety net, as well as allow her to accumulate funds for a future down payment on a condo or house.

- Aggressively continue paying off credit card debt over the next ten months. Once those are taken care of, redirect funds into the money market account.

- Purchase some inexpensive term insurance, with a face amount of $500,000, to lock in insurability for the future, as well as provide her with the peace of mind that her family will be taken care of. This policy can be converted to a permanent policy in the future.

- Secure a private disability insurance contract to supplement the group coverage provided at work. This will bring the amount of income replaced closer to what her monthly expenses are. Also look into adding a future purchase option, which will allow her to purchase more coverage as her income increases, without proving insurability.

Capital Accumulation Stage:

- Continue participation in her employee stock ownership plan at a level of 5%. This will provide her with a medium-term investment that can be used for a down payment or any other future needs that arise. Over the next few years, we will begin investing in mutual funds to further diversify this portfolio.

- Purchase a variable adjustable life insurance contract, contributing $75 per month to this plan. Again, this will lock in her insurability as well as provide her with the potential to create a living benefit within her life insurance plan.

- Consider purchasing a house or condo in the next few years. She can continue to live with a roommate to help keep costs down.

Tax-Advantaged Stage:

- Consider lowering her 401k contribution from 10% to 6%, which will still allow Jillian to take advantage of the full company match, but free up monthly cash flow to help pay off the credit cards and get other aspects of her plan in motion.
- Begin participation in a Roth IRA, which will provide Jillian with potential tax-free income at retirement.
- Roll over her 401k from her former employer into a brokerage account IRA rollover fund. This will give her control over the investments she chooses. She could also roll to her current 401k, but she would like the options to pick and choose any stock or mutual fund instead of being limited to the current choices.
- Based on a risk tolerance assessment, Jillian has a long-term growth profile. She is comfortable taking on some short-term volatility for potential long-term rewards.

Summary

Due to the life experience Jillian has had, she has a unique appreciation of the importance of protecting her family at a relatively young age. Saving money is also important to her, so she spends her free time learning about real estate to educate herself on her upcoming home purchase. Instead of shopping, she's paying off her credit cards and looking over *Home & Garden* magazines browsed for free at the library...imagining the fabulous furniture she will buy for her new home once she can truly afford it. She is at a point in her life where, by living frugally, she is going to put herself ahead of the curve both in short-term life goals and long-term financial security.

Case Study #2: Single First-Year Pharmacist

Nick finished pharmacy school six months ago and is working at a local retail pharmacy. He is single and just purchased his first home. Nick envisions himself getting married in a few years, with children to follow. Nick had various part-time jobs while in pharmacy school, which allowed him to contribute to a Roth IRA. He was fortunate enough to have his undergrad completely paid for through scholarships. Although Nick enjoys a nice lifestyle, he is concerned he is not allocating his income as efficiently as it should be.

Nick's primary goals:

- Plan for retirement.
- Establish short- and medium-term savings vehicles.
- Eliminate credit card debt.
- Invest and manage his Roth IRA.
- Lower his tax liability.
- Protect his income and future insurability.

The Numbers

Nick enjoys working at ABC Pharmacy and for now sees himself working there his entire carrier. He understands this is his first job out of pharmacy school and would like his plan to work no matter who his employer is. He is paid $46 per hour and, with the occasional overtime, anticipates his income to be roughly $103,000 this year. Nick has access to the standard employee benefit package that includes health insurance, disability insurance of 60 percent of income capped at $6,000 per month, life insurance of one times salary, and the ability to contribute to a 401k (after the first year). The company will match 50 percent of his contribution up to 6 percent of his income. His monthly take-home pay is $5,500, and his monthly expenses are $3,500, leaving $2,000 per month in excess funds with which to plan.

His Net Worth Statement

Fixed Assets:
      Savings Account: $10,000
      Checking Account: $6,000
      Total Fixed Assets: **$16,000**

Variable Assets:
      Roth IRA: $22,000
      Mutual Funds: $12,000
      Total Variable Assets: **$34,000**

Personal and Other Assets:
      Home: $220,000
      Vehicle: $20,000
      Personal Property: $15,000
      Total: **$255,000**

Total Assets: **$305,000**

Liabilities:
      Mortgage (5-year ARM at 7%): $205,000
      Credit Cards (12%): $4,000
      Auto Loan (7%): $18,000
      Student Loans (3.5%): $65,000
      Total Liabilities: **$292,000**

Net Worth (Assets Minus Liabilities):   **$13,000**

The Financial Plan

Security and Confidence Stage:

- Purchase an umbrella liability insurance of $1 million, including liability coverage for uninsured/underinsured motorists.
- Immediately pay off credit card debt with funds from savings account.
- Establish a money market mutual fund as his emergency reserve instead of the savings account. Contribute $250 per month. Continue to build up the emergency reserves to reflect, at a minimum, three months of fixed expenses ($10,500). Transfer most of his checking and all of his savings account to this.
- Supplement current long-term group disability plan with an individual policy.
- Secure life insurance using a combination of heavily funded variable adjustable policies and term insurance.
- Pay an extra $250 per month towards his 7 percent car loan.

Capital Accumulation Stage:

- Initiate an investment advisory account utilizing a diversified portfolio made up of 80 percent equities and 20 percent bonds. This is considered a "growth" portfolio and was determined to be suitable after a risk adversity analysis. Contribute $500 per month.
- Fund a variable life policy, but keep this within the limits allowed by the IRS so it does not become a modified endowment contract. This provides another opportunity for tax-favored growth for retirement, while also addressing his life insurance needs. Contribute $500 per month.

Tax-Advantaged Stage:

- Restructure the Roth IRA to reflect 90 percent equities and 10 percent bonds. Nick's prior allocation was made up of only 30 percent stocks. It is currently unclear whether Nick will qualify for the Roth IRA for this year. If he can qualify, he should continue to fund it.
- Once he is eligible, contribute to the 401K up to the company match.

Speculation Stage:

- Hold off on this section of the plan until the base is more established.

Summary

Nick's new plan addresses all of his goals as he outlined them. He will lower his taxes, free up cash flow, save and invest wisely, and plan for his future.

He likes the fact that his risk management needs have been addressed. He is much better protected in all aspect of insurance and has a foundation with which to build on. This gives him much confidence knowing he has options and choices, should he decide to change employers.

He also has a much better understanding of where he is at financially (net worth) and with his cash flow (budget). His plan balances all aspects of the financial pyramid, and he feels prepared for the next phase of his life. In the meantime, he will continue to build up his investments and review the plan periodically with his financial planner.

Case Study #3: Young Married Couple with Children

Circumstances: Steve and Joan are both thirty-two years old and have two children, ages four and one. Steve has just changed his employer. He is an attorney in a law firm, and Joan was a school teacher until the couple had children. The family lives in a New York metropolitan area suburb. Their financial situation is as follows.

The Numbers:

- Steve's annual salary: $150,000
- Net monthly income: $10,000
- Company-sponsored life insurance for Steve: $375,000
- Steve is making maximum contributions to his 401(k), and his firm matches 50 percent up to the first 6 percent.
- Balance on home mortgage: $350,000
- Monthly expenses: $9,000

Assets

- Steve's 401(k) balance at previous law firm: $49,000
- Joan's 403(b) balance: $11,000
- Approximate equity in home: $300,000

The Financial Plan:

The couple asked us to review their financial situation and make suggestions for improvement. Steve and Joan completed a questionnaire to determine their "investment profile." Joan is "conservative growth," while Steve is an "aggressive growth" profile.

Our first suggestion was that they apply for a home equity line of credit to use in the event of an emergency, since they have no liquid assets. Even though Steve is an attorney, the family does not have a will or any of the other estate planning documents. We emphasized to Joan and Steve that drafting these important documents should be a priority for providing a plan for their families.

Next, after reviewing their insurance coverages, we suggested the following:

- Steve should apply for a $2 million life insurance policy using a twenty- or thirty-year term coverage with a policy that allows a disability waiver of premium clause. Also, the policy should be convertible to a permanent policy. Joan should do the same for $1 million of term. The amounts of coverage were determined using a capital needs analysis approach.

- Since Steve's group disability coverage is paid for by the employer, the benefits are taxed if and when received. Therefore, an individual policy should also be purchased to better protect Steve's entire take-home pay.

After a review of their budget, and their determination to monitor expenses a bit more than they have been, they determined together that they could commit $1,500 a month to their financial plan. This would include premiums for the life and disability insurance, and a monthly savings plan to include:

- Maximizing individual Roth IRA accounts while their adjusted gross income permits
- Establishing an interest-bearing account where they could have money transferred each month from their checking account. This savings account will be used as an emergency fund.
- Establishing two individual 529 College Savings Plans for the children
- Rolling over Joan and Steve's retirement accounts presently held at their previous employers to individual self-directed IRA accounts
  - ➤ Our suggestion for Joan was that she reposition her 403(b) into an annuity contract that provided a guarantee to comply with her "conservative growth" profile.
  - ➤ For Steve, we suggested that he roll his 401(k) into a fee-based account utilizing a portfolio of no-load mutual funds with objectives that would meet his "aggressive growth" profile.

Case Study #4: The "Sandwich" Couple

The "sandwich generation" is a term that has been coined to describe the many baby boomers who are in a similar situation as Marilyn and Gene, "sandwiched" between caring for children while also trying to care for aging parents. Marilyn is forty-three and is a university faculty member at a prestigious university. Gene, age forty-six, is a successful small business owner. They have two daughters, ages nine and eleven. Up until this point, they have handled their financial planning themselves, but with increased work and family obligations, that has become too challenging.

Their goals include:

- Pay for their daughter's higher education expenses and weddings.
- Determine the correct amount of life insurance they need.
- Review the cost of health care for the employees of Gene's business.
- Look at the available options to help parents during retirement and long-term care needs.
- Make sure they are on track to enjoy a relaxing retirement that includes travel.

The Numbers

Their monthly net income from all sources is $30,000, and their monthly expenses, both business and household, amount to $22,000. Their home has a market value of $1,500,000 with a $760,000 mortgage, and the estimated value of the business is $600,000.

Net Worth Statement

Assets:

Bank Savings Account:	$10,000
Business Checking Account:	$47,000
Gene's Qualified Plan:	$235,000
Marilyn's Qualified Plan:	$180,000
Joint Brokerage Account:	$8,000
Home:	$1,500,000
Personal Property:	$200,000
Total Business Value:	$600,000

Total Assets: **$2,780,000**

Liabilities:

Mortgage:	$760,000
Car Loan:	$4,000
Business Debt:	$44,500

Total Liabilities: **$808,500**

Net Worth (Assets minus Liabilities):   **$1,971,500**

The Financial Plan

Security and Confidence Stage:

- A comprehensive review of their insurance revealed many gaps that needed to be filled. We advised that they work with their current property and casualty insurance agent to add a $2 million umbrella liability insurance policy. Also, they increased their deductibles from $100 to $500 and added excess umbrella liability coverage for uninsured/underinsured motorists.

- They moved their short-term money (personal and business) into a money market mutual fund instead of the savings account at the local bank. This increased their yield while still providing them the needed safety and liquidity. They also paid off the car loan and freed up the cash flow from that payment.

- They purchased private disability insurance to better protect their greatest asset: their ability to earn an income. They increased their life insurance with a combination of a base of permanent coverage utilizing a variable adjustable life policy, and supplemented that with a sizable twenty-year term policy. The needs were determined using a needs analysis program to identify the minimum coverage they needed, and then increasing that need towards their "human life value," which is the maximum amount an insurance company will issue on them. Because so many people are counting on them, Gene and Marilyn wanted to err on the higher side of coverage.

- They also discussed at length the subject of long-term care insurance on their parents. Fortunately, Gene found out his parents did purchase long-term care insurance policies many years ago. But those policies did not have a cost-of-living escalator, so they purchased a second policy to supplement the parent's policy. Marilyn's parents did not have any coverage, but their fixed income during retirement doesn't allow any surplus funds in the budget. Marilyn approached her two sisters, and the three of them agreed to split the cost of the long-term care insurance policies on her parents. They decided it was easier and more prudent to budget this expense, rather than leave this risk exposed. Everyone in the family is glad that a plan is in place for any long-term care needs of their parents.

Capital Appreciation Stage:

- Since they have a sizable monthly surplus ($8,000 per month) and no more expenses to cover (they were putting money into their home, buying cars, and even feeding some money into Gene's business by taking a lower salary for years), they are now in a position to start saving aggressively.

- They started a 529 College Savings Plan for the girls' college education and will be adding $500 a month to each account. They are over-funding their new variable adjustable life policies to take advantage of the tax-deferred compounding, and they are adding $4,000 a month to their brokerage account. Ultimately they are going to build up a diversified mutual fund portfolio that could be used for extra college and/or wedding expenses, or a supplement to retirement.

- Gene is also working hard to build a management team at the business. He realized that while he was self-employed, he really just had a job. The business would not run without him, as he has not become comfortable with delegating key decisions. So, to "buy some flexibility in his schedule" and build more value in his business so he could sell it someday, he knows he needs to give up some control and begin to train and empower his key employees.

- Additionally, over the next few years, he will "employ" the daughters for help with basic tasks around the office (e.g., mass mailing projects, basic filing, even cleaning and emptying the garbage). This gives them a chance to work together, as the plan is to go into the office for a few hours on the weekend, earn a little spending money, learn the value of hard work and responsibility, and fund a Roth IRA for the girls, just to get them started on the right path financially.

Tax-Advantaged Stage:

- They will continue to fund their qualified plans at the maximum level. In addition, Gene is considering a class allocation profit-sharing component to the 401k he provides, so as his business continues to grow and thrive, he will be able to add more to his plan.

- They added a health savings account as part of the employee benefits review. Moving to a higher deductible group health insurance plan, they saved some costs and shifted 25 percent of the family coverage to the employees. So the health savings account is another way of putting some money away on a pre-tax basis to help cover future health-related expenses.

• Through a questionnaire that assesses risk tolerance, a diversified growth portfolio was developed for the qualified retirement assets. Up until now, they chose funds at random, gravitating to whatever had done well the year before. Now they have a system for periodic rebalancing and reviews with their advisors.

Summary

Both Gene and Marilyn are very excited about their experience working with a financial planner. While the process did take some time, they are convinced it was worth it. They are better prepared for all of life's contingencies, and they have a regular savings plan to achieve all of their financial goals. Since seeking our advice and staying on track with their plan, which includes annual reviews, Gene and Marilyn feel confident they are on the right path to fulfilling their financial dreams.

Case Study #5: Semi-Retired Couple in Mid-Sixties

Mary and Patrick are in their mid-sixties, and Patrick is working part-time doing consulting work in the industry from which he retired. Mary worked for five years after college at the phone company. She has been a homemaker since their children were born. They have three children, Ryan, Brendan, and Ian, ages thirty-eight, thirty-five, and thirty-three, respectively. Brendan and Ian are each married, and each have two children of their own. Ryan lives with Mary and Patrick, as he has a special need, severe Autism.

The Numbers:

- Patrick's Annual Consulting Income: $60,000
- Social Security Monthly Income (not yet receiving):
  Patrick: $1,400
  Mary: $700
- Patrick's IRA Value: $900,000
- Mary's IRA Value: $140,000
- Joint Brokerage Account Value: $270,000
- Tax-Deferred Fixed Annuity: $172,000
- CDs and Money Market: $55,000
- Home (no mortgage): $450,000
- Patrick and Mary each have $100,000 of W.L.
  (life insurance in place for more than twenty years).

The couple asked us to review their investments, their retirement income plan, and their estate plan. Mary and Patrick would like to live their desired lifestyle, which they have been doing on Patrick's consulting income. They would like to know how they could continue to maintain their lifestyle after Patrick stops consulting, and still be able to leave enough assets available for:

- Their senior years (eighties and nineties)
- Ryan to be able to live the lifestyle to which he has grown accustomed (Anticipated annual income need for housing and living expenses is $50,000 per year on top of what he receives from Social Security each month.)

- Making certain Ryan is taken care of after Mary and Patrick die
- Leaving something for Brendan, Ian, and their families**

** Mary and Patrick are somewhat frustrated that the only way to take care of Ryan after they die is to put *everything* in a trust for Ryan and therefore leave *nothing* to their other two sons and four grandchildren. They know "that's life," but it doesn't make them feel any better. They do not believe there is an "equal" or "fair" solution.

Planning for Retirement Income:
Investments/IRAs/Savings:

Mary's $140,000 IRA is heavily invested in various low-yielding individual stocks she has acquired as a result of various splits, spin-offs, mergers, and acquisitions. A small portion of her IRA is invested in a diversified mutual fund. For the most part, Mary has "inherited" an IRA portfolio as a result of the activities in the financial marketplace rather than proactively building and maintaining an appropriate portfolio relevant to her time horizon and risk tolerance.

We evaluated her investment comfort level and applied a "conservative growth" investment strategy using diversified mutual funds instead of her individual stocks. We used a fee-based brokerage account IRA to transfer in her old IRA in-kind. Once the assets were transferred, we sold her old stocks (with no taxes upon sale because they are in her IRA) and built a suitable IRA portfolio for her (more diversified and potentially higher yielding). We recommended she let this grow for now and begin distributions in the future.

Patrick's $900,000 IRA is the sum of four IRAs in separate places: two smaller 401(k) Rollover IRAs from previous employers, and two larger IRAs that represent an old cash balance plan and a pension plan that was "rolled out" to employees. When asked about his reasons for not consolidating his IRAs up to this point, Patrick said he did not want to "have all of his eggs in one basket." After conversation, we explained "his eggs" would be diversified and better managed if held together "on the same farm" or in one diversified, properly allocated IRA account.

Consolidating his IRA accounts into one fee-based brokerage account (similar to Mary's) made sense for all of the reasons listed above. In addition, Patrick is getting closer to age seventy and a half, where at that time he must begin taking required minimum distributions from his IRA in order to satisfy the rules of the Internal Revenue Code. The IRS will levy hefty penalties for required minimum distribution amounts not taken from IRAs each year. We oversee that this is done properly, and it is simpler to calculate and take required minimum distributions from one IRA as compared to having several.

Patrick went through the same risk tolerance evaluation Mary did. Patrick, as a result, we discovered is slightly more conservative than Mary. We built/allocated his portfolio with an emphasis on "income and growth." When he stops his consulting work, most of the household income, $60,000, will be drawn from this IRA each year.

Mary and Patrick's joint brokerage account is comprised of various stocks and some municipal bonds, but mostly it is comprised of two large-cap mutual funds. Generally, the growth on this account over the years has been okay, which is good. However, at this point in Mary and Patrick's lives, they could use more diversification to preserve what they have accumulated. A greater income emphasis from this account (with some growth) would also better assist their cash flow.

They agreed an "income and growth" strategy here would make the most sense. We transferred the account "in kind" and then, with capital gain taxes and losses in mind, we repositioned the account to a more suitable portfolio. A small portion (less than one-half) of this joint account's annual earnings will be used to pay annual premiums for their long-term care protection plan (discussed later).

The tax-deferred fixed annuity of $172,000 is in Mary's name. This account was created as a result of an inheritance she received from her mother Marion's estate. When her mother passed, she left Mary $150,000 with her three grandsons in mind; $50,000 each, if Mary did not need the money herself. Beyond that, Marion left it open-ended and up to Mary to decide. Mary deposited the $150,000 into a fixed annuity she obtained through her bank. She would rather not ever touch this account. Mary would like it to grow and leave it to her three boys "from their grandmother." If absolutely necessary, she would like access to any dollar value over $150,000 in future years.

Based upon Mary's risk tolerance ("conservative growth") and her intentions for this tax-deferred fixed annuity, we suggested she transfer the fixed annuity to a variable annuity with investment sub-accounts linked to the equity markets for higher upside growth potential rather than only earning 3 percent, which is what the fixed annuity was offering. We accomplished this transfer to the variable annuity with no income taxes by using a 1035 exchange. Also, we utilized a rider on the variable annuity to protect the principal from loss in the event Mary dies when the financial markets are down. This way, the three boys would be guaranteed the initial deposit (less withdrawals) or potentially more, even if the financial markets brought her account down substantially.

Mary and Patrick love this idea, because it enables them to invest these assets for growth, use this savings if needed, and preserve Marion's intentions.

Planning for Senior Years (Eighties and Nineties):

Planning for Possible Incapacity and a Long-Term Care Need:

Mary and Patrick are concerned about their less-active later years in life (their eighties and nineties). They want to be certain they have adequate funds to live and maintain purchasing power. Also, they want to protect themselves from the possibility of a long-term care need. Patrick does not see this "happening to him" and believes a policy will be entirely too expensive. Mary is also concerned about where premium dollars will come from; however, she wants as much control (and choice) in life as possible.

We recommended a shared long-term care policy. This policy has a four-year benefit period beginning with $150 per day. Should one person use all four years, they could use the other person's benefit as well, if it is available at the time. Often, shared care plans are more cost-effective than individual plans, and this helps keep the premium lower. This plan provides some flexibility in where care will be delivered, and it includes home care.

Depending upon the degree of incapacitation, the $4,500 per month ($150 per day for thirty days) may pay for all or part of the care needed. Any additional funds needed Mary and Patrick would pay from cash flow and savings.

This long-term care plan gives them a solid base of coverage and is far better than owning no coverage and assuming the entire risk themselves. The premiums for this plan will be paid for once a year out of annual dividend and portfolio income. Paying the premiums this way will not interfere with their monthly budget.

<u>Estate Planning:</u>

Leaving a Legacy to Their Children and Grandchildren while Delivering a Promise to Ryan:

Mary and Patrick have always maintained up-to-date wills, power of attorney, and advance directive documents. However, there was a "not entirely clear" special needs trust in their wills. There also wasn't a funded trust in place. After a qualified estate planning attorney reviewed the documents and made improvements, Mary and Patrick's instructions were more transparent.

The purpose of the special needs trust is to designate (for Ryan) assets outside of the taxable estates of Mary, Patrick, and Ryan. This is done to maximize the value of Ryan's Social Security income eligibility and preserve the assets to be used over his lifetime.

The legal documents were now up to date, yet we still had more work to do. In order to achieve the objectives of providing for themselves, for Ryan, and disposing of their estate as fairly as possible, we implemented a $1,000,000 second-to-die life insurance policy. The policy would be owned by Ryan's special needs trust, and it would be funded through annual gifts from Mary and Patrick. The annual gifts to the trust would then be used to pay the premium for the policy each year.

"But where would the annual gift money for the special needs trust come from?" It was time to begin taking the Social Security retirement income.

"We'll use your Social Security income today to create and secure Ryan's income for tomorrow." When either Mary or Patrick die and the smaller Social Security income is lost, we will use the proceeds from the $100,000 whole life policy (that each of them have) to cover the death-time final expenses and offset the loss in Social Security income.

Even though Patrick was slightly overweight and a diabetic, we were able to successfully get the coverage in place. One of the major benefits of a second-to-die policy is that the premium is typically lower than the premium for two individual policies. This is because the second-to-die policy pays one death claim at the *second* death.

Mary and Patrick were amazed this could be done. They did not know this kind of life insurance existed. They activated their Social Security income (which they had not been using), used it to make annual gifts to Ryan's special needs trust, and when they both pass on, Ryan's trust will receive $1,000,000, which will be prudently invested to deliver Ryan approximately 5 percent, or $50,000, per year.

Now something (the remaining value of their IRAs, home, savings, etc.) could be left for Brendan, Ian, and their four grandchildren.

Summary:

We gained an understanding of Mary, Patrick, their family, and their objectives. We were able to make some improvements to their investment and IRA portfolios to better position them for their active retirement years, their less-active senior years, and the years thereafter when they are looking down on their family: their boys and grandchildren.

They were both relieved on various levels and admitted they did not think so much effective planning was even possible. Now, they can live! They have comfort knowing that some productive financial planning has been implemented and that their goals will be met.

11

Additional Resources

Glossary

Annuities,
Fixed

A vehicle marketed by an insurance company that pays a guaranteed rate of return.

Annuity,
Variable

An investment marketed by an insurance company with premiums mostly converted into separate accounts invested in stocks, bonds, and money market accounts.

Assets

An investment or property that has value.

Those assets that do not have a major loss of principal. These would include the most conservative assets in your portfolio, like checking and savings accounts, money market funds, certificates of deposit, T-bills, EE savings bonds, and whole life insurance cash values.

"Bear"
Market

A period of time in which securities are declining in price.

"Bull"
Market

A period of time in which securities are rising in price.

Capital

Money or other assets.

Certificate of Deposit	An account at a bank, savings and loan, or credit union that pays a fixed rate over a certain period of time.
CFP®	A Certified Financial Planner™ is a person who advises others on achieving long-term financial goals, either for a fee or on a commission basis. Ethics and professional standards are monitored by the CFP® Board (www.cfp-board.org).
ChFC	Chartered Financial Consultant—a degree earned through the American College.
Debt	Owing money.
Diversification	Spreading your risk among various accounts to reduce volatility.
Dollar Cost Averaging	The buying of a fixed dollar amount of stock shares at regular intervals so that more shares are bought at low prices, fewer at high, resulting in an average cost that is lower than the average price.
Inflation	A period of time marked by rising prices.
IRA	An individual retirement account.
Liquidity	How easy it is to convert your investment into cash.
Money Market Mutual Fund	A pool of assets invested in bank CDs, T-Bills, and commercial paper, and considered the best emergency reserve account due to safety and liquidity.
MSFS	Master of Financial Services. An advanced degree earned by the American College.
Mutual Fund	A general term for an open-end investment company compromised of investments in basically any category.

Portfolio   A listing of securities held by an investor or organization.

Principal   The current balance owed on a debt or the value of an account.

Securities   Investments.

Stock/Share   A certificate representing ownership in a corporation that is usually sold to raise money to begin or expand a business.

T-Bills   Treasury bill, a short-term federal obligation of the U.S. Treasury sold at a discount.

For Further Information

The following is a very brief list of some of the resources for the individual interested in personal financial planning. To list all the helpful information available today would be a book in itself, so included here are some of the most popular and my personal favorites. The opinions and strategies expressed in the following sources should not be acted upon without first discussing them with a qualified investment, tax, and/or legal advisor.

Newspapers

The Wall Street Journal is the most widely read business newspaper. It also has daily articles about investing and money matters.

Barron's is a weekly newspaper that reviews the stock markets. The Lipper Analytical Services mutual fund performance ratings are included on a quarterly basis. There are also frequent articles on mutual fund investing.

Investor's Business Daily is an excellent newspaper with a broad range of articles on finance, business, and the economy.

The New York Times and *USA Today* both have excellent business sections.

Magazines

Money magazine's December, January, and February issues usually have articles on tax and investment planning.

Kiplinger's Personal Finance magazine's January issue focuses on financial planning (including tax planning) for the coming year. Mutual funds are reviewed in the September issue.

Smart Money offers articles on investing and financial planning.

Forbes is a biweekly investment magazine that looks at news from an investment point of view and has an annual mutual fund survey usually published in August.

Business Week focuses on current business news and contains articles on personal business, investing, and financial planning.

Books

Golf Is Not a Game of Perfect by Bob Rotella has nothing to do with financial planning. But since I'm addicted to the great sport of golf and am always trying to improve, and see others improve, I recommend this book any time I get a chance. It provides some great ideas on the mental side of the game.

The New RetireMentality by Mitch Anthony is a great new book that identifies the issues facing everyone as they plan their future. This is especially helpful to those who are worried about what they will do during their retirement years.

There's No Place Like a Nursing Home by Karen Shoff is a must-read book for anyone who needs more education on long-term care for themselves or their loved ones.

The Ultimate Gift by Jim Stovall provides a very interesting story about wealth and the transfer of wealth to the next generation. I would suggest this book for anyone who wants to instill a sense of values and work ethic into their children, employees, and others.

Web Sites

www.toddbramson.com is my Web site and has valuable links to many financial sites, including many of those listed below.

www.wallstreetcity.com has just about everything you need to know about stocks, including free quotes, research, and criteria-based charts matching your specifications.

www.investorama.com lists information of thousands of online financial sites.

www.quicken.com includes a wealth of personal finance information, as well as calculators and interactive financial formulas.

www.bloomberg.com offers financial market reports.

www.sec.gov is the official site of the Securities and Exchange Commission.

www.savingforcollege.com discusses the multitude of state 529 college plans available and each of their advantages.

www.morningstar.com features a comprehensive review of mutual funds, and portfolio tracking.

www.savingsbonds.gov lists everything you need to know about U.S. savings bonds.

www.irs.gov provides information on the publications and forms for most tax questions.

ABOUT THE AUTHOR

Certified Financial Planner™ Practitioner Todd D. Bramson has been working in the field of financial planning for over twenty-five years, and has been recognized as one of the 150 best financial advisors for doctors nationwide by *Medical Economics* magazine. He is one of only forty-seven financial advisors who have been listed each of the last five times *Medical Economics* has provided this survey. An exceptional teacher, as well as a motivating author and speaker, he has been quoted in numerous financial publications, and has spent several years as the financial expert on the local NBC live 5:00 p.m. news broadcast. In June 2004, he spoke at the prestigious Million Dollar Round Table, a worldwide organization of the top one half of one percent of all financial services professionals.

Mr. Bramson's belief, "If the trust is there, the miles don't matter," has earned him devoted clients not only in his hometown of Madison, Wisconsin, but in multiple states throughout the country. Along with all the advanced degrees expected of a trusted financial professional, he is committed to keeping abreast of all the developments in his field, and to playing an active role in his community. He conducts regular public seminars and is active in the Evans Scholars Alumni Foundation, and Blackhawk Country Club.

Mr. Bramson is also the founder and president of Bramson and Associates LLC. Information on his company, philosophy, and services can be found at www.toddbramson.com. You will quickly see that Mr. Bramson is dedicated to providing valuable wisdom through his books, Web site, presentations, and newsletters.

NORTH STAR RESOURCE GROUP

Todd D. Bramson, CFP®, ChFC, CLU
North Star Resource Group
2945 Triverton Pike Drive #200
Madison, WI 53711
1-608-271-3669 ext. 218
todd.bramson@northstarfinancial.com

TRN: 109116
DOFU: 10.09

ASPATORE